# HOME ORGANIZATION: 2 BOOKS IN 1

# ORGANIZING YOUR HOUSE

# DELCUTTERING HOME

The Best Practical Tips And Ideas On How To Clean Your House, Keep It Organized And Get Rid Of Stuff You No Longer Use

All rights reserved. © 2019 by Anne Marie Rooms.

No part of this book may be scanned, uploaded, reproduced, distributed, or transmitted in any form or by any means whatsoever without written permission from the author, except in the case of brief quotations embodied in critical articles and reviews. Purchase only authorized electronic editions and do not participate in or encourage electronic piracy of copyrighted materials. Thank you for supporting the author's rights.

**Disclaimer**

All the material contained in this book is provided for educational and informational purposes only. No responsibility can be taken for any results or outcomes resulting from the use of this material.

While every attempt has been made to provide information that is both accurate and effective, the author does not assume any responsibility for the accuracy or use/misuse of this information. Some names have been changed and/or omitted in order to protect the privacy of certain characters in this book.

# ORGANIZING YOUR HOUSE, THE SIMPLE AND COMPLETE GUIDE ON HOME ORGANIZATION

*The Best Practical Tips And Ideas On How To Clean Your House And Keep It Clean*

# Contents

Introduction ............................................................................................. 4

Chapter One ........................................................................................ 12

Removal .............................................................................................. 12

Chapter Two ....................................................................................... 20

Assessment ......................................................................................... 20

Chapter Three .................................................................................... 35

Preparation ......................................................................................... 35

Chapter Four ...................................................................................... 43

Drawers .............................................................................................. 43

Chapter Five ....................................................................................... 53

Flat Surfaces ....................................................................................... 53

Chapter Six ......................................................................................... 62

Project Organization ......................................................................... 62

Chapter Seven .................................................................................... 71

Accessibility ....................................................................................... 71

Chapter Eight ..................................................................................... 89

Storage Volume ................................................................................. 89

Chapter Nine ...................................................................................... 98

The Small Stuff .................................................................................. 98

Chapter Ten ...................................................................................... 113

Creating Storage Space ..................................................................................113

Conclusion..........................................................................................127

# INTRODUCTION

*"Cleanliness is a state of purity, clarity, and precision."* -Suze Orman

You get home from work one day, and you find your home upside down. The floor has crumbs of dried mud on the floor, you find your laptop on your sofa, your books aren't neatly placed in the bookshelf, your shoes are scattered in the living room, and when you reach your room, it's worse. There are piles of clothes and shoes all over the place. You are about to scream your voice out, but then, you remember it's just you living alone *in this* house. Yes, I know that feeling, and I know what it takes to clean it up and put every object strewn around back to the right place.

The truth is that no one likes a disorganized house; even kids don't like it, but they still mess up the house. Same way with you: you wake up early in the morning to start the day's job, but even after choosing your clothing the previous night, you decide to change your outfit, and before you know it, outfit after outfit, you change, throw it around until you find the one you like.

But have you ever realized, just as people have a bad hair day, people can also have an issue with what they will wear. Yeah, a bad dressing style day, and so it can have you throwing your clothes here and there. If you're an organized person, then you wouldn't have a problem with what to wear because you must have ironed it the previous night. The big problem is that, as much as a lot of people don't like a disorderly house, a lot of people also hate cleaning up the house. Not just that, but keeping up with the constant cleaning can be a major problem. Laziness is one of the biggest problems! And you have to fight it. Good thing for you, 'organizing your home' will put you through every detail you might need to get you started.

Cleaning and organizing the house definitely doesn't top a lot of people's to-do list of activities. I mean, who sits down to write down their schedule and then add: *10 am, Tuesday (house cleaning)*. I'm sure you will find it exceptionally weird. If I stumble upon someone's note and find that in their schedule, the first thing that will come to my head is: "Wow, this person is very detailed."

You probably think, "Yuck, cleaning is too much sweat!" Yes, you are right, absolutely right. But have you ever realized that, the more you clean up regularly and arrange your living arrangement, the easier it is to stay in an organized environment? Okay, pause; you probably didn't get what I mean. The issue is that most people wait until their house turns out to be a big mess and end up being too dirty before thinking: "Oh, yes, I should clean up my house." A lot of people keep junk and stuff under their beds, in the closets, and drawers, and when it's not fully arranged, it gets messy and becomes a problem. Doing this will certainly cause you hours of cleaning and organizing, and as much as this book is meant to help you in the areas of organizing your home, doing the right things, like returning an object to its original position after usage, is super important.

Before you delve deeper into this book, I want you to answer a question truthfully: Is your home dirty right now? I know you may probably roll your eyes and say, "Duh, isn't that why I got this book?" You are baffled and you keep trying every way possible to keep your home clean and always arranged. I presented the question above so that you can acknowledge deep down in your heart the problem you are facing in your house. But don't you worry. Accepting there is a problem when there is truly a problem is the first basic step on your journey to a clean sparkling home. There are so many things that you may be doing in your home that is causing the whole big mess; trust me, I've been there, and I have the experience to teach you better. Or, sometimes, it is not just a *'you'* problem it is a *'what'* problem. What exactly is in your home that is causing so many problems? Do you keep too many piles of paper and books on the desk in your room? Do you return your makeup brushes and lipsticks to your purse? Like I mentioned, the ultimate point is, do you ever return things back to where you took them? Where do you keep your dirty clothes? Are you are married with a kid? Learning to make your home neat is the way to go. You don't have to dread going back home to a pile of dirty dishes or clothes.

Read through this carefully and do not omit any part because everything I'm about to tell you will take you far, and it will keep you from the stress that comes with a dirty environment. There are ten things I have learned over the years when it comes to ways to organize your home. These ten things are the ultimate guide. If you follow them, you never ever will have a problem with a disorganized home again. Remember a clean home can bring you happiness!

**1.    Removal**: Like I mentioned earlier, there are places you've been keeping unnecessary things in your home. Books that aren't important are lying on your study table. Have you ever thought of putting them in a box or giving them away? Remember, I did not mention throwing out things that are important. This tip is mainly for every object that causes a disorganized home.

**2.    After every unnecessary object** in your house has been removed, you need to look around your house. You know your house better than I do. You need to find out if there are things that might be helpful for you to store things in your house. One thing I always put into use when cleaning up my home is to look for things that can be used for storage. Even that old mug can be used to store your pencils if you are an artist. Just analyze it; anything can end up being useful.

**3.    Preparation**: So, you've made your survey, you've found things that can help you store the important things in your home, so what do you do next? You should prepare for the arrangement in your home.

**4.    Drawers**: One of the amazing things about storing your things in one container or another is that a container is not the only thing that can keep the space in your home clean and organized. I have drawers in my home, and they are readily available to store things for me. Particularly, my towels and other lady things. My point is, drawers come in different sizes, shapes and numbers. Some can also be attached to your dressing mirror.

5.  **Flat Surface**: I have been to houses where they stack their dining tables with books, papers, and other objects that aren't even food related. The dining area should be clean and clear of any type of object. Its purpose is just for eating, and once that is done, you clean up. The dining table isn't the only flat surface area in the house that has been misused by people. Flat surfaces can be used to add an aesthetic touch to the house, but anything other than that is a no.

6.  **Project Organization**: Now that the first few things about cleaning and organizing your home have been addressed, then you should put your cleaning in a schedule book. You might hate to spend the whole day cleaning your house. You are not alone; I hate that too. By planning for cleaning ahead of time, you'll get more time to find objects you want to give out, throw out or keep. So, start right away. Label your storage with a marker or stick a paper on the container to remind you the purpose each container or storage will serve.

7.  **Accessibility**: I know, as you make plans for making your house clean and organized, you must really feel happy about that, but one thing you should keep in mind is that every object stored in a safe place should always be easily accessible. You don't want to store your

pens in a container only for you to have forgotten where exactly you put it. Oh, yes, I have made that mistake before. I kept my things in a container, only for me to rip my room apart again just because I was searching for that important piece of clothing. There are other times I have stored my items above my closet and needed to get to it. Having a stool or ladder that can be folded will go a long way.

8.     **Storage Volume**: It is vital to watch the volume of storage in your home. Movement from one place to another shouldn't be difficult for anyone, so you need to keep the volume of storage at bay. This reduces your stress of moving around your house.

9.     **The small stuff**: I always have a tape, pen or pencil around. Don't blame me; I'm addicted to jotting down every important detail. But do you know the easiest place to keep my small items if I'm being too lazy? I just dump it on a table in the living room or the dining table. Which is totally wrong. These small things constitute a lot of mess in the house, and that is why I mentioned above that small containers are very useful in the home. They can be used to store these small things.

10.     **Creating storage space**: Keep in mind that there are spaces in your home that can be used as storage areas. Have you checked the space above your closet? What about under your bed or staircase? Keep in mind that, as you read on, you will learn lots and lots of things to keep your house sparkling clean and organized.

So, I put it up to you one more time: is your home clean and organized? Before I proceed with the helpful details that will help you for as many years as possible (even when you are married or have kids running around), have you ever wondered why it is so important to have your house clean. I mean, aesthetically, it is vital for you to make your house look as beautiful as possible, but sometimes or most times, it's not only about the beauty that comes with cleanliness; it's about living a healthy life. It's about being able to locate your things easily or keeping yourself safe from home accidents.

Look, organizing your house has thousands of benefits. I can go on and on about the benefits, but the thing is that I won't go too deeply so as not to bore you. I will show you a few benefits then let you think about it.

In life, there are things you know how to do from day to day, which reflects on other parts of your life. Have ever wondered how people with good saving habits do things? I'm of the opinion that, if you are an organized person, then you will know how to save money. People who are not organized will keep buying duplicates of things they already have in their house. They keep buying these things because they know they need to have those items, but they forget that, if they are not organized, they'll keep losing their items. Now, I will only add one more point about been organized before moving to the next chapters.

Dust, mold, and the rest of the 'dirt' family can cause real health issues. So, dust your things and get them arranged. Trust me, you don't want to fall because you spilled water on the floor and then land on a hair brush. So stick around and keep reading. In the chapters below, I will go into details on the solutions to a dirty apartment.

# CHAPTER ONE

# REMOVAL

*"Cleaning and organizing is a practice not a project."* –Meagan Francis.

Not everyone knows what to do when it comes to organizing their homes. Most times, it can be tiring and frustrating. Yes, I've been frustrated in the past when I didn't know a thing about cleaning and arranging the house. It was more like a trial and error task for me, until I did my research and tried these tested tips I'm about to teach you. You see, these are interesting secrets to home cleaning, and they make the task look like child's play. Yes, cleaning the home can be difficult. You've not had a good experience with it, but I'm putting this out to you right now: forget about your horrible experiences with cleaning. Just look at it this way and tell yourself: "I didn't know the secrets to cleaning up the house." If you sort everything in your house, you will realize it is not that difficult to organize your home.

In order to arrange your things effectively, you should know how vital it is to check out your storage options. Most times, people automatically believe the garage is the only space to keep unimportant things. But it doesn't have to be that way. Even a garage can be neatly arranged. Your major aim here is to search your house and start removing cupboards, racks, containers, shelves, and anything available both in and out of the house. You can either repair these storage options or replace them with better ones that are free of insects (termites). Sometimes, the storage options you have at home can be useful in other rooms, so don't just remove them from their confined spaces and throw them out. Make sure you are certain of their usefulness too. You never can tell how grateful you'll be for listening to your cleaning *instincts*. One thing you must know is that, getting rid of bad storage options will give room to a new one or even a spacious living environment.

I have derived several storage solutions, and believe me when I say it works like a miracle. If you take a closer look at the carton of shoes boxes in your garage, it can be very useful; a glass cup storage solution can be important as well. One thing you should take into consideration when removing is to note that anything can be used to store things in your home. Sometimes, that one object you think is useless is not. Look deeper and think outside the box.

I want you to do one thing right now because that's what I do when I'm about to think of creative ways to make my home pop. Step out of your house for just a minute. If you have a garage, look through it. What storage solution did you find? Yea, I'm guessing a shelf, maybe some cardboard boxes, drawers or a television stand? In the past, garages were mostly, if not only, used to park vehicles. But have you ever noticed that, even in movies, garages are usually filled with so much junk that even a car can barely be parked in it. What is more challenging is to know how to store things in it or knowing what is useful in your garage and what is not. You need some garage ideas, but that will be discussed as you continue to read this book. In my previous book, I generally discussed ways to *declutter* your home, but I know you are not reading this for the purpose of *knowing how to declutter*. You've probably cleaned it out, but now you want to find ways to identify those storage solutions.

Did you know, after I carried out this practical tip, I found so many storage solutions for my stuff at home? That space in your ceiling can be very useful to keep ladders or fix a garage shelf. That space under your staircase can be used to keep numerous things. Do you have a cabinet you think is not useful to you anymore? Take it out and think of ways you can turn it into a useful shelf (that is, if it's not completely ruined). Or you can it and find a suitable wire shelf, preferably an open shelf that would give easy access to any item. Once you are able to purchase or remake an open shelf that shows all your items, you'll be careful enough to keep it clean and arranged.

Put it out first. Then go back into your house and study the living room. What is out of place? Do you have your television placed on the ground? Are you a bookish nerd and your books are everywhere in your living room? Is the TV remote lying around with nowhere to be kept? It all depends on how disorganized your living room is, but you own that place, and you know what is out of place. Right now, I imagine you need a TV stand, probably a book shelf or a table.

Sometimes, a TV stand with drawers can be useful to store compact disks and remotes.

Once you are done surveying your living room, did you find any broken storage solutions there? If you do, remove it and find a replacement or send it out for repair. There are times I have made repairs myself just with a hot glue gun.

Now, go into your room and do the same. I am certain you will definitely find some things, in fact a lot of things, out of place in your room. The aim here is to remove these things and think of ways to repair them, remodel them, or throw them away. These are practical methods I have tried, and I encourage you to try it too. The first time I ever did this, I realized I had tons of cardboard boxes: from telephone boxes to shoe boxes, nails, etc. Did you know there are so many do-it-yourself things you can make out of cardboard boxes just for storing your things? Yes, that's right.

I realized the purpose of my shoe boxes is not just for littering my whole room. I was able to gather decorative papers, leather straps, metal braids, and hot glue and turned my useless shoe boxes into storage for craft supplies, jewelry, and makeup brushes. Although, I really do not know much about you, as you read this to get your home organized, you really need to get handy and step up. About any useless thing can work for a storage option in your house. All you will need is a few bucks to get tools and supplies for joining and dismantling. For example spanners, hot glue, nail, screwdrivers, and hammers are a great way to take your storage ideas to another level. So, look around right now and gather something. Who knows what you might need to throw away or gather to create something fantastic?

So, are you sure you've checked out things you need to remove, replace, or repair in your bedroom? Now, get into your kitchen and find out why your plate is just lying around on the kitchen cabinet. Your pots are right there at the top of the cabinets too. What about your cooking ingredients? Do you have the spoon *neatly* placed on the plates? You and I both know that is not the rightful place. Now, think of new storage options that are useless and throw them out too and replace them. You see the keywords for this method are the *R* words: *Remove, Repair and Replace.*

It means to repair objects that have been removed. Like I said, removing objects is a crucial step to take if you ever want to get your house in order. Experts believe so because that is one of the early steps they take before doing anything in organization. I'm of the opinion that throwing out things that might eventually serve as a storage option isn't a smart move. You might think: "Oh, but it's broken." Look here, some things can be fixed! Glues, nails, soldering iron can fix a lot of things. I'm giving this advice to you because it will help you save money for future purpose. Imagine throwing away a cupboard just because the door got broken? What are your nails for? You don't have an hammer? Then go get one from the store. If the handle of your drawer is ripped off from weakness, then get a nail and fix it. Don't waste your resources by throwing away and buying new things every time just because it is broken. Okay let's take a look at storage solutions you can fix in your home if they are not completely broken:

- Plastics can be fixed with a soldering iron.

- Cupboards can be fixed with nails or hot glue.

- Buckets, yes, I have used buckets to store Christmas decorations in the past. They can be fixed with a soldering iron.

- Containers (if metal) can be fixed by spray painting if it's not completely damaged.

- Shoe boxes, if torn, can be fixed with a simple cello tape. The list goes on.

If your storage solution is permanently damaged, then you can always replace it. But don't just go on a spending spree. If you only want to store small stuff, then you should learn the containers that go well with it. If you are storing big items, then know the storage solution you want to buy. That is the purpose of removing, doing project organization, and making preparations. It will be bad for you to blindly get storage solutions without actually needing them. Are you going to get a cupboard just because you need to store small stuff at home? I'm guessing your answer is no. Never ever make that mistake of getting a storage option without knowing what purpose it will eventually serve.

There are a lot of benefits that come with the removal of storage solutions:

1. Removing old storage solutions gives birth to a new spacious home.

2. Removing old storage solutions can bring new ideas to add aesthetics to the house.

3. Removing old storage solutions to create or replace them with new ones can be stress free for you. The easier the access to your things, the better.

4. Removing old storage solutions to be replaced or repaired creates a safe space in the house to keep your things from lying around the house.

5. There is this serenity that comes with a good space for storage. The world out there is lousy enough and with too many people going about their business; removing, replacing and repairing your old storage solutions for a better version will help keep the house clean. A clean house equals a great deal of calmness.

6.     Removing your old storage solutions to be replaced with a better version keeps the house clean and will help you be ready at any time to have visitors around your home.

7.     Removing your old storage solutions to repair can actually save you money from buying new ones, so if you do not go around checking things out, you will never know.

8.     Last but not the least: Do you know that removing a storage solution for a better upgrade will help you store your things? Yes, I know you already get that part. But in order to store things that you can give out, you really need to start cleaning right now. It simply gives you quick and easy access to your things.

Do not leave any of your things lying around. Moving onto the next chapter and do not forget to carry out that practical step of looking around your home right now.

# CHAPTER TWO

# ASSESSMENT

*"You don't get anything clean without getting something else dirty."*
–Cecil Baxter

In the previous chapter, I discussed extensively the first things you should do on your way to having a clean and organized house. If you are an extremely organized person who loves putting everything into place, you might want to take out your notes too. Is it every part of your house that needs reorganizing? Or is it just one part? Alright, hold on a minute. If every part of your house needs reorganizing, have you listed things you'll need to store your clothing, makeup, books, jewelry, and TV remotes, stationary? If you have not done that, start doing it now. It's time to step up your cleaning and organizing game.

After every poor or ineffective storage option has been removed, replaced, or repaired, it's time to examine how you use the remaining or upgraded storage solutions. Changing how you store the items in your house may lessen the need to get new storage solutions. For example, in the kitchen, are your most commonly used items, cutlery, plates and cooking items, easily reachable? Rearranging the storage of these high-use items will give you a more enjoyable experience in the kitchen. Using space well will provide more space for new storage options. So, look at how the furniture is organized in major parts of the house, such as the kitchen, living room, and bedrooms. If reorganizing the furniture uses available space better, this could provide more options for storage options later. There are ways that furniture will be arranged and would give space for better things to be put. I have tried it in situations where I arranged the furniture in my house differently, and believe me when I say it didn't only change the outlook of my home, but it also created space for more things to be neatly organized. Doing this will be intimidating to do. But seriously, rearranging the furniture has its benefits. Arranging your house furniture will give it a new look. What other makeover do you need in your house? So try something new, push your sofa to the wall, change your glass table to another side, and every other thing will really help the look of your home. It will create the illusion of a spacious home.

Rearranging your house will make it look like it's even neater. I mean, if you do not have your furniture jam-packed together, don't you think your house will look neater? Check out houses with a minimalist tone. Have you ever noticed how the furniture looks? Do you know such apartments have fewer furniture and always end up looking very neat? Well, that's the trick, and that is the point of rearranging your furniture.

Another point of rearranging your furniture is to create floor space. You get to have a walk path without knocking your legs on any furniture. So, look around your home, not just your living room, and see the things you can do about the furniture. Repeat this rearrangement throughout your home. But before you do, I'll take you through the process of assessing and making use of available storage options from the garage to the kitchen, the bedrooms and living room.

1. **Analyze the garage**: When you imagine the ways you will go about organizing your garage, you may wonder if you also need to spend tons of money. But ask yourself first; hasn't it been a while since you parked your car in there? If that is out of the way, then it means more space has been created for you. And if you've followed my advice on removing, repairing, and replacing, you may not necessarily spend so much money. One thing is for sure, if you've surveyed your garage, you will find some useful storage solutions lying somewhere on the floor of the garage, begging to be put into good use. So no, you do not need to spend much on storage solutions because, like I advised, you have taken the first step to a clean, healthy home. Worry no more. Here's how to arrange your garage with little or no money:

- Organize first before thinking of ordering a new one. A lot of people have made the error of going to a store to buy tons of containers hoping to hide their problems. Yes, I call it a problem because having your important items lying around the house is a big problem. So, yeah, back to my point. A bunch of containers won't solve the problem with your unclean house. In fact, when you pile your house items into a container, there's a big chance you will find it difficult to get your things easily. We don't want that, do we?

Before you buy anything, check through your garage. Usually, people keep garden tools, sporting gear, and mechanical tools. Now, I need you to take your garden tools and put them aside. Keep doing that with every tool of the same purpose until everything in your garage has a category. I would advise you to arrange according to size, but trust me, that method has been tried, and I failed woefully doing that. I can't have the rake and a golf club stored in the same place; it makes absolutely no sense, so if you are already thinking of arranging according to size, then please stop. Let the tools go according to the functions they perform. If you find any tool that has been damaged, toss it aside.

- Have you ever pictured your garage as a small space? I know you probably think "but my garage can contain a car?" Nope, that's not what I think. I'm telling you to picture your big garage like it is small. How will you arrange it in a way that will make it look good? Do you get what I mean? Like I mentioned above, keep a tall, open shelf. It can be wooden or metal. The reason you need a tall shelf is to arrange your things in an upward motion, and an open shelf will teach you the benefits of being organized. So, yes, start arranging your items on the shelf. Put the items you don't use often up on the top shelf, e.g., Christmas décor. You can also get them with ladders that can be folded.

- Now that you've pictured your garage as if it were a small space, it's time to know the part of your garage where the shelf will fit. But, have you ever thought of using pegboards. If you are handy, you can make one yourself or find someone to do that for you. Using a screw to drive it into the wall of your garage is also advisable. Add hooks to the pegboard to hold your garage items. The one mistake I first made while making mine was not using something to hold the hook in. Get hot glue and glue it up.

- I have mentioned this in chapter one, but it doesn't hurt to remind you again. Are you standing in your garage? Do you see the old furniture covered in dust? Do not throw your furniture out and call it useless. No wood is useless, except if the termites got to it. So, check out the drawers of that dusty furniture and change it into something you can store your things. Do not let your thing go to waste just because it's been long since you used it or because it is covered in dust and you assume it is ruined.

- The type of person you are depends on the things you have in your garage, but let's say you have a bicycle or objects as big as a bicycle. You can find strong hooks (strong enough to hold bicycles) and get ply wood. Have it hammered on the garage walls.

2.     **Analyze the bedroom**: If you are like me, you follow lots of pins about *DIY*. In full, DIY is do it yourself. Do it yourself projects are a very common thing on Pinterest, and sincerely, they will help you in this rearranging project you are about to embark on. I have done a lot of do-it-yourself storage solutions more times than I can count, and I tell you this; sometimes, you do not need to spend a dollar to reorganize your home. One of the best things about trying to do it yourself is the aesthetic effect it can add to your bedroom and home in general. Something as useless as a crate can work as a storage solution and still beautify your home. All you might need is paint, some glue (if you will be using decorative papers) and glam it up. Like I have advised from the beginning of this book, not everything is meant to be thrown away.

But how do you find the best storage solutions for your bedroom? You don't have to think too hard because this is why I wrote this book in the first place. I have filtered through tons of ideas, gone through different Pinterest pins, watched YouTube videos, and studied different things in my room, and I realized one thing: you do not need to go broke just because you want to organize your home. Now, let's get down to business and see how you can organize your room with these useful hacks.

- Fix shelves on the top of the walls. The most vacant spot of the house is the wall just below your ceiling, but have you ever thought of storing things up there? So, get handy right now and put something up in your room or find someone to fix that for you.

- I had issues with my cords for charging phones and my tab. Seriously, I hated the fact my chargers were left on the floor, making my room disorganized. One of the things I came up with one day, while I was on my computer typing away, was clip binders on my desk. These things are not only portable, but they can be useful to clip your chargers in place and create space in your room. Besides, getting your phone chargers tangled can ruin them. This is one of many ideas for storage solutions when starting with small spaces in your bedroom. So attach it to a charging box and voila, you have your phone chargers and earpiece tucked neatly away from the floor.

- Is your closet full? Then take up the space in the corner of your room, make a rack, and hang it on the wall.

- The headboard in your room can be used for storage. Hopefully, if your room is just a bed and clothes, then you should take that chance to make use of it as a storage solution. Your bed can be modified to store more things. Instead of having a cloth rack, you can create a storage option in your bed and store your clothes.

- Do you have your laundry basket taking up too much space in your bedroom? Then I think it's time for you to find a solution, such as hanging a laundry hamper behind the door in your room. See why you need to analyze your space to find somewhere for storage?

- When I explained surveying your garage, I mentioned finding a purpose for your old things. A crate can be used for your shelf; even a bad radiator can be painted and used to store books. That is where removing and inspecting old storage items in your home come to play.

- You can take wood from your garage, stack up some things, and create a floating shelf.

This particular step is very important on your journey to a clean house. Analyze your room very well; you never can tell what idea you might have to allow enough space.

3. **Analyze the kitchen**: One of the benefits of analyzing your home is to help you notice what you are doing wrong and then visualize things better. Are you using the space in your house efficiently? Do you know that using your space well, reorganizing it, and removing useless storage solutions will provide more space for new storage solutions? No one likes a kitchen that has little or no storage options. Picture it this way: a kitchen with no cabinet, not even a table. No container for ingredients, no plate rack, fridge for storing raw food or veggies, no cutlery rack. Just a stove or any form of cooker, pots are left on the floor, how would you even cook in an environment like that? Look, you need to get thing working and

arranged in your house to create easy movement, and now is the time to do that.

- First, have you ever thought of what a vertical arrangement will do for your kitchen? Back in high school, that was one of the things I learned. Various ways to arrange your kitchen. Look, it's not that technical; in fact, it's not technical. All you need to do is either arrange everything in your kitchen, including the cabinet, in a U-shape or L-shape. But the downside is that this only works best if the cabinet is detachable. So why don't you just try a vertical storage pattern on your kitchen walls. Think a wooden or stainless metal slab (in form of shelf) to lay your cooking pots neatly. This will help you make use of the space on your kitchen cabinet, especially when you need the flat surface on your cabinet for other important things.

- Try using the space around your fridge. Have you noticed there is a space between your fridge and the wall? Maybe it's time you make use of it. Don't let any space go to waste but always thing aesthetically. You don't want to turn your space into a mess after trying to organize it. I found a rolling pantry from Alan Chu, and it's absolutely amazing for keeping canned foods and other nonperishable, edible items in your kitchen (think hot dog, tuna, corn beef etc.)

- I realized you don't need to have a container to keep your cutlery. There is a great idea for you to keep them clean and dry. A stainless pegboard, like the idea I mentioned for your garage, can go well for the kitchen too. This will actually save space in your kitchen and make it look organized but aesthetic. You don't want to have a yellow painted kitchen and get an orange peg board attached, so as you think of a space, consider the beauty that comes with rearrangement.

- While thinking of super great ideas for organizing the home, I stumbled on a picture with a curtain covering a small, secluded room. This room looked too small to work as a room, but you could spice things up and revamp it into storage. Have someone hang up some wooden objects or metal and create a shelf in that small space. Have slabs set up horizontally and store some canned foods there. You don't necessarily have to create a space in the kitchen; it might be anywhere around the home. Just have a nice curtain covering it and voila, a beautiful storage space.

- Try using the corners of your kitchen space; it'll go a long way. Putting cupboards on the walls of the kitchen is a great idea for storage. The major thing you want to achieve here is to get your things off the kitchen cabinet and use the walls, which is a great idea. In fact, having things on your wall is one of the most suitable ideas to get enough space around the home. Keep this in mind.

- Stop putting your wine on the table around your kitchen. Not only will it give an untidy outlook, but if it falls, you'd have to start cleaning up. Why not find a stylish wine rack?

- You have wine everywhere, and then you have a fridge. Instead of looking for ways to store your wine, why not just find a way around it in your fridge or put it in the storage idea I wrote previously? Both work well and keep the environment in your kitchen clean.

4. **Analyzing the bathroom**: One of the places people mostly ignore around the house is the bathroom, well apart from the garage. You see, I know the bathroom is only meant for bathing; it's not as if you get to spend your whole day in it. I agree that the living room is the most used area of the house and the room, but you don't want to have a dirty bathroom just because you feel it's not that important. In fact, I'm going to be touching on two aspects of cleaning the bathroom: the cleaning itself and then organizing it. But first, let's analyze the ways your bathroom can be organized. Do you see your sponge stuffed by the bathtub or bathroom window? Do you think your bathing lotion shouldn't be left by the edge of your bathtub? I think the same.

- There's usually a space under the sink in your bathroom. This space is just there, with nothing to put there, yet you have your dry towels strewn over the door. It's so bad you can't even keep your bathroom door closed, right? Why don't you have a metal or wooden small shelf fixed below your sink? You can neatly fold your towels there.

- If you think that might be too much for you, how about going back to your garage to find that ladder? Be it wooden or metallic, I'm guessing you know the right store to get spray paint. Why don't you have it painted and use it in your bathroom. This ladder can serve as a good spot for hanging your towels. If you think it'll protrude too much, it's time to shave off the extra wooden surface and make it flatter. Either way, it'll give your bathroom an aesthetically good view while helping you organize your bathroom.

- Two slabs, wooden or stainless, can be useful to keep your soap, body wash, and electronic toothbrushes. So, now, take up that space on your bathroom wall and make use of it.

- Have a laundry basket under your sink just for your towels and other bathroom wears. The space on your toilet is wasting away. Why don't you find a flat basket and place rolls of toilet paper on it? Remember aesthetics and space!

- Fix up a magnetic strip on the wall for your blades, tweezers, and bobby pins. Don't leave these items on the edge of your sink.

5. **Analyze the living room**: Every part of the house can present arrangement challenges, even the living room. You know, the part of

your home where you spend the most time. I believe, if you live alone, then you probably spend a lot of your time in the living room watching the television and doing other things. So how will you organize these things in your living room? The layout in your living room is absolutely important when it comes to making any form of arrangement. Where are the spaces in your living room where you store things? Do you use any drawers? Let us take a look at ways the living room can be analyzed in order to create storage solutions.

**Never leave any angle in your home untouched:** Don't be sad about a clumsily shaped place, slanting roof, or a weird structural detail. Instead, take advantage of the odd corners and less used area for storage spaces in the sitting room. That is the point of analyzing what you have in order to create a better version of it. The most interesting storage options for strange angles in a home contribute to a lot of things, and you can boost the area, so you know it's worth bringing skilled people to help you look at it. Once you've drawn the ideal choice, detect an excellent cabinet builder to reconstruct it for you.

Tables are awesome: This is quite **basic,** though a practical idea for bringing storage options instantly. Change your table, that is if you have one in your living room, into a shelf that can serve a multipurpose. It takes no extra impression, and it's ideal for any kind of books, newspapers, magazines that may not look good on a shelf.

**Every corner is important:** Don't disrupt your storage options because you think a corner isn't good enough. A common shelf system can be created to be attached to the walls and can create more space in your house, and they even look more fascinating than two open-shelves in the open space of your home. Even though you might be staying in a rental apartment or you have a stiff budget, it is a good idea to look for shelves that are already made and specifically constructed for corners of the house.

**Have you ever tried a low cabinet**: The thing is, when you make proper investigations, you will know what part of your home needs a corner cabinet, what part needs an actual shelf, and what part will work with a low cabinet. Cabinets that are low will make a room airy, and it will still be a good and accessible storage section for your home. When there is space in your house, especially on the walls, now it's time to take note of that because, with such space, you will have a great number of storage solutions with minimal impact on the way that room actually looks. The surface will definitely create an excellent space for showing off your home decorations.

If you can't detect a good storage solution from the store to go well with the space in your house, then you can change other cupboards to the size or shape you want. It's all about making a part of the house that will go well with the design of your home and the dimensions.

**A work desk will work fine:** A work area is now progressively relevant, but a lot of homes usually won't have the space for the extravagance of a detached work room. A small table is a great space to store things and still give you space to work. Cabinet, cupboards, and drawers can keep all, especially files, hand towels, and candles.

# CHAPTER THREE

# PREPARATION

*"A new broom sweeps clean, but the old broom knows the corners."*
–Irish Saying

Effective storage in the home is vital so that you can arrange your home and your items in good condition. Remember the first tip I mentioned. For you to make your house clean, you must first clean out, remove those storage options you might put into use, and throw out the ones you won't need. Have you ever wondered about ways to store your things? In fact, it has become a problem for you but not to worry. I have you covered. And I have constantly made the point above that, in order for you to create storage solutions in your house and create space, you must also think about aesthetically pleasing ideas. Arrange for easy access to items in your home so as to use space efficiently. Your major aim is to keep creating space without making your house look like a mess. There are many different places in your house that probably need to be utilized if you pay proper attention and do something about it. You need not search for advice from hardware stores or renovation companies for any ideas because that is what I'm going to teach you. Just sit back and pay attention.

I encourage you to take your phone right now and google search minimalist living room. Instead of clicking on all the or news icon, click on the images and marvel at the beauty of the minimalist living room. First of all, for those of us who want to understand the clear meaning of a minimalist living room, here's a simple meaning: The minimalism approach to housing décor is a design that is categorized by austerity and laconism in decoration. You see, this kind of design in homes is done through the use of furniture and simple colors, and if you want to add geometric shapes to it, then it's fine. The truth is most, if not all, minimalist designs are very plain colors, like brown, white, black or grey. Who knows, maybe navy blue can be used, but it is a design that provides serenity, and that is exactly what I'm trying to get at. What tone are you trying to set up in your house? All these things are things you should consider when preparing to organize your apartment. A minimalist house rarely looks disorganized. I'm not saying you have to change the look of your apartment, but if you have some bucks to spend, why not?

For you to have an organized and clean apartment, you must make preparations. Ask yourself these questions: Am I only cleaning and organizing my house for the sake of it, or am I doing this for aesthetic purpose? No, scratch that. What's the point of reorganizing your house if you are not picturing a beautiful vicinity? The first thing that should come to your mind when visualizing where you want this particular item or that item to go is to imagine if this rearrangement will bring beauty to your home.

You really need to start on a clean slate, and to do that, preparations are necessary. Yes, you've taken a step, and one of the first things you've done is getting this book to know what to do and how to do it. Write down exactly how you want to make your apartment look, start listing tools you'll need to make it look neat, write down things you already have that will give you the effect you are looking for, start doing everything to prepare for what you want for your house.

Do you want your sofa to back the window or face the window? Where would you want to place your TV? Would you want your remotes next to the TV, or do you want to find somewhere to keep them? If you do not prepare for this step, you might not get it right. Look at your apartment again. What style is the interior? If you've gotten the style it is, search pictures of a neatly organized house and see what you can make out of it.

Are you going to be using the vertical method of storage to keep enough space on the ground? Write it down; it's called being organized. Preparation equals organization. No matter how many details you get down when starting to organize your house, imagine not preparing at all. "What do I need to do before arranging my home?" is a good question. Remember that.

Once you've removed, this stage will make you know what you truly want. Do you want a well-ordered, stocked storeroom or a cotton closet with the flawless volume of space to keep folded bedspreads and towels? Find what's significant in order to make sure your house includes all you need. Another reason you should prepare for organizing your home is to keep track of all items you'll need, so that when you bring all the items that will be useful for storage, you will just label and tick off the items. All in all, the amount of preparation you will need depends on the number of rooms in your home. So start now and get busy with your home décor, cleanliness, and organization.

I want to take you through ways to see organization. You see, when you look deeper, you will understand the point of organization and how to fix it. Let me ask you something important, which I want you to answer truthfully. When asked to explain what an organized house looks like, what would you say? I believe most people will have a good explanation. I believe people will say it's clean and well-kept; some will ultimately think it's boring. No, I don't necessarily think a minimalistic house is a boring house though.

A space that is organized is far beyond that. I have seen houses that are neat with no drop of dust on the surface, but it's just on the surface. When you go deeper into their cabinets, you see nasty, dirty looking things, and then you wonder why the outside is so neat. Okay, let's forget neat now. Do you know your study table can be neat on the surface, yet the drawers are packed with so much stuff that is not even organized. Did I strike a chord? I bet the answer is yes.

I have seen people who live in a house where its items have spiraled out of control, yet they do not feel uncomfortable until they start looking for important things. How do you find things? How do you live in an environment where you can't easily pick something just because you are not organized? Now let me put it out to you: An organized home is the environment created by people who live in it. In this environment, people have everything arranged systematically while giving access to items in the house. An organized environment naturally makes you feel relaxed.

Having an organized environment takes a lot of skill and practice. Still, it is a very easy skill if you practice it well. To get everything right, you need to make preparations. Preparation starts with you researching online, going to hardware stores and renovation companies to find storage solutions that are great yet aesthetically pleasing. How do you know what is good and what is bad? Research, research, research. Keep finding ways to get your house in order.

The most necessary elements of an organized house is a living space with enough storage. Do you get my drift? Look, having your household items littering the floor, table and kitchen is very easy to make it look less pleasing when it comes to aesthetics. The best way to get these things in order is by preparation for the project ahead of you.

Have you checked your house to know what part of the house need a certain storage fixture? You can't just buy things you do not need because, if you do, you end up losing money. If you still don't think you need preparation, then let me take you through the process of preparing for a project and why I think organizing your home is a project.

Before you embark on any project, you will always be advised to prepare. For example, if you want to write an exam, will it be advisable for you not to read? Well, I think not. It is highly advised for you to read in order to succeed. Now, liken it with the process involved in organizing a home. If you do not make preparation, organizing your home is bound to end up in a mess. Now, go out there to renovators, draft plans, meet people, go to YouTube and find out ideas. Yes, you've started that process, I guess. That's why you are reading my book.

Draft a schedule that will show when exactly you plan to finish your project. This planning will now determine the route this organization will follow. It will determine if money will be spent or not. So what is your objective? Do you want to finish this quickly? Then I advise you to start preparing for it. Sometimes, it can be normal for a project to change its direction because that is the quality a good project has: flexibility. Just because your project takes a new direction doesn't mean it is a bad project. Believe me, it is not. Let's say, for example, you have made plans to get eight containers for storage but then, after removal, assessing that all stems from preparation, you realize five storage solutions are enough. This wouldn't ruin your chances of successful planning. Organizing your home can only end up in a mess if you never considered making any plan or preparation.

You need to start by knowing what really works for you and what doesn't ever seem to work. Ask yourself questions; analyse your home situation. What are the things you don't have a place for? Is it your nail polish? Do you have a home for your keys, your documents and so on? All these questions will only pop up when you do your assignment and prepare for the project ahead.

I have learned in many years, when it comes to organization, you must think of a plan for the future. Have you started with a picture of what you really want in your head? This process involves visualization, thinking of what you want, and how you want your house to look.

Like I have mentioned and will keep hammering on in the course of this book, organization isn't getting rid of clutter and creating a *surface neatness*. It is greater than that. Organizing is a skill everyone should learn. You design your space, and it looks systematically arranged; you design your space in a way that makes it easy for you to take things easily then that is all it takes to be organized. In fact, having an organized place reveals who you are. I have numerous methods, and I will be sharing one in particular that I use when it comes to making preparations before the actual project.

- Method one of preparation: We all know the kitchen is basically for food preparation, washing dishes, dish storage, and food storage. Now think of what each individual tool performs in your home and prepare towards finding ways to store each kitchen tool into groups. Do you have tools for just cutting or for cooking or for dishing plates? Start making preparations on how you want them stored. The earlier, the better for you. The point of this method is to take note of the items in your kitchen, bathroom, living room, garage, bedroom that deliver similar service.

My point is, you need to prepare. I'll keep repeating it until it sticks and you get the point I'm trying to get across. You need to learn one thing. When a home is organized and conducive for people living in it, there's a greater chance of actually being active in important activities. Your spaces will allow working or reading effectively.

# CHAPTER FOUR

# DRAWERS

*"The objective of cleaning is not just to clean, but to feel happiness living within that environment."*

So, you've made your preparations, you've researched storage ideas, you've gone to stores to check the kind of containers that are best for your house to keep them organized, but have you stopped to think of the drawers? Drawers are really lovely storage ideas, and I promise, in this chapter, you'll learn how to utilize your drawers properly. But do not make one mistake: throwing just any item into each drawer randomly. Don't feel bad if you've been doing that though. People make mistakes, and it's about time you learn how to do things right. But before you go about arranging your things in your drawer, you need to do it and be sure your items will be easily accessible.

Some people call it chest drawers, dressers, or cabinets. Although I think calling it a cabinet is not a befitting name, the basic point is that drawers are very functional and can be put to good use if you have a good eye. Drawers were designed for storage purposes in times past, and they've been there to give your home space with the edge of an aesthetic purpose. It is an issue of fulfilling two major things a home should have: beauty and aesthetics.

You see, drawers can be used in any part of your home. If your living room, kitchen, bathroom or bedroom doesn't have a cabinet, then you're really missing out, and I wonder how you've been keeping some drawer-worthy objects at home. These wooden or metal structures can present aesthetics through designs and size.

You know that a wooden drawer that might have been changed into different things, even into a wardrobe, will always remain a very good storage solution for your home. In the olden days, drawers mostly were used to keep clothes and up till now, you still hardly see a bedroom without a drawer. It's like it has been set to default: bedroom and drawers go together.

Drawers are believed to be very necessary in the bedroom, and I totally agree. These days, people use drawers in every part of the home and are now believed to serve more than the purpose of keeping clothes.

Most drawers come in rectangular shapes and are usually not more than five feet from the ground. This method of furnishing usually comes with one or two drawers. Things keep changing, and the methods of furniture and home decorations in general will keep changing. These furniture structures are mostly made of wood, and you know how wood transforms a place to a beautiful abode. But who knows? You can make drawers from other materials that aren't wood.

Being different can be unique, but while at it, study the durability of the material you plan to use.

Just as other furniture, wooden drawers started a very long time ago in medieval Europe. Then, they called it a wooden box that came with or without feet. Oak trees were cut down, chiseled, hammered, and joined together with nails to make this type of furniture.

There are different ways the drawers can be styled. Drawers have been refinished and polished then passed as furniture with a tinge of vintage style. They can be designed in numerous ways. I love the finishing that comes with painting the chest drawers. Imagine having a flowery wall paper decorated house with a blue painted chest drawer: aesthetic plus a good storage solution.

Integrating a drawer into your apartment is a great way to improve the look and feel of your house. You can use a small drawer for a nightstand table in your bedroom as a space to keep a lamp and an alarm. It can even work as a side table when they are next to a beautiful sofa. This way, you are going for both a beautiful look while storing your things neatly.

Drawers serve a lot of purposes. I will tell you this again and again. In the course of this chapter, I will take you through ways you can use drawers in every part of your home.

Keeping the kitchen storage of your home arranged and operational is very fulfilling, and it can be difficult to decide where to keep a lot of kitchen items, most particularly if you've been making use of the same kitchen for a while now and you are already used to it. You have to know that it will be wise to keep the items you use the most at chest height for easy access. The items you use less can be stored higher or lower. So let's start small and step right back into the kitchen and see what can be done with those drawers.

**Ways to store items in the kitchen drawers/cabinets**

1. Egg slicer, knife (any type of knife) etc. You know the cutting tools you have in your house, and it is better to store these cutting tools in a section together so that, whenever you want to cut something, you pull out the drawer and pick your cutting tool.

2. Depending on your cooking habits, you can actually store the common items you use in your kitchen in the same place.

3. You can keep the rarely used objects together. Do you have items you only use during a special event, like thanksgiving or Christmas? Then it's advisable you keep them separately in another cabinet.

4. You can put your pans and pots in a very imaginative manner. You can hang your pots and pans on hooks on the wall, but since we

are talking about drawers here, why don't you store it below in the cabinet?

5. Get new organizers for your kitchen cabinets. The moment you have decided the sections you would prefer to keep your kitchen items, find the corners in your kitchen where your cabinets will need extra arrangement and tools for storing things.

6. Large cabinets are aided with roll-out shelves, including home-made or ones bought in a kitchen or organizing shop.

7. Do you know woven baskets can make up for drawers? In fact, they actually do look like drawers. How about for a change, you get a bunch of woven baskets, put them in a large shelf, and store your kitchen items in it?

8. I was bored one day, and I decided to scroll through YouTube, and I stumbled on a decoration channel. Thankfully, not only were other parts of the house mentioned, the kitchen especially was talked about. The average drawer is especially very good for cutlery, but other kitchen utensils can be difficult to put in the such drawer; they do not come in the same size and not all people have similar kinds. In that particular video, they talked about using a bunch of drawer dividers, not a plate. If the dividers are used, one can create different sizes of the storage space you want. What's even better about dividers is that you can find the ones that are adjustable. The dividers that are adjustable can be enlarged to fit in the kitchen drawers.

9.	In order to retain your organized kitchen and easily find kitchen utensils, you should put a label in the cabinets or even outside. This would easily tell you where the spoon or the knife is.

10.	I found a corner cabinet in a friend's house, and believe me when I say I loved it! Do you have parts where your kitchen items are shifted to the back of the cabinet? Is it always difficult to reach those kitchen tools? Fix a turntable and enjoy easy accessibility to your kitchen items in the cabinets. It is actually more suitable for items you don't use from time to time.

**Ways to organize things in your bathroom drawer**

Getting your bathroom drawers arranged neatly will definitely save you so much time when preparing for your daily activities. You know why? You will be able to find things easily without stressing yourself. But wait a little bit. Before diving into organizing your bathroom items, consider arranging it into different categories. It is this step that helps you further. Using dividers for drawers will keep them in place and separated from one another. But if you have organized your drawers constantly and you still haven't found enough space to keep your bathroom items, you can always relax and learn.

1. Get everything out of your drawer. You can place it on a towel or a counter space; just get everything out. This step makes your work faster and easier.

2. Try categorizing all your bathroom items. Group these items.

3. Arrange your drawers using a divider. Drawer dividers are really helpful when it comes to separating products into sections. This makes everything easy for you to locate without stress and keeps your drawer section very organized.

4. Put your most used items in the top drawer. So start sorting out the things you use every single day. Do you use your cream every day? Yes, put it up there. If you have a particular lipstick you love so much, it's the time to put it up for visibility and easy access.

5. It is advisable to store your largest items in the compartment with the widest space. It is not sensible to try to stuff your less used items in a small compartment anyway.

6. Put other products or items you have in their own compartment. Store products of different functions in their own space. Do not make

the mistake of placing rarely used products over ones that are used daily.

7. Another way to make use of something similar to drawers is to keep your products in a medicine cabinet. Most medicine cabinets have a transparent door or a door that serves as a mirror.

8. You can find a really beautiful basket-perhaps when you are out of drawer space-and keep your items in it. The baskets can easily be placed under a bathroom sink.

**9.** Keep your items in a trolley. Store your things in it however you like. You can place smaller products above or just place products you use the most on top of the trolley layer.

**Ways to organize every other drawer in your home**

1. Organize all the drawers in your home. There are various tips that will make it absolutely easy, and that is why I have created this separate section just for utilizing the drawers in your home. I'll tell you the truth; I have arranged lots of drawers, especially in my home, from drawers in my bathroom to the ones in my kitchen and bedroom. I'm used to arranging them and upgrading to a better, more

fashionable version. My major concerns when organizing my drawers is to determine the best ways to keep things neat while still maintaining beauty and easy accessibility. Have you ever wondered how to organize your dresser? I use the folding method. It doesn't only beautify its outlook, but you absolutely don't need to start through the drawer before getting the clothes you need.

2. Another reason I encourage the method of filing folded clothes is that it gives access to modification and alteration. You can arrange your clothes according to your size.

3. The drawers in your bathroom can be arranged, but it can also be difficult due to the fact that they are usually deep and narrow, and it may cause a fall and ruin every arrangement you've made. So, a drawer divider that is a good size for the bathroom will be needed. Just like every other drawer, you can use acrylic bins in the drawer not only to divide it, but it can be used to store different things depending on their sizes and items you want to store. You can actually keep your nail polishes according to colours if you're willing to go all the way or just stick to one bin per similar objects. You can store your hand sanitizer or hand cream. You can get a larger bin in your drawer for towels.

4. You can add more bins to store more items, like pens, pencils, rubber bands. The truth is that those bins can store items that you use for your interests.

5.     Do you work from home? Do you have an office in your home? Then start using the ideas you used in the bedroom to arrange your things in the office.

6.     Have drawers built under your bed. It is a very good idea to store your clothes or towels, even use it to store cosmetics.

# CHAPTER FIVE

# FLAT SURFACES

*"Cleaning is therapy for me. I'm not ashamed of holding the duster or broom."*

Many people are guilty of what I'm about to discuss in this chapter. Even I have gotten carried away. Flat surfaces are not storage locations. I repeat, flat surfaces are only meant to contain decorations, not storage options. There are so many flat surfaces in the house, from dining tables, kitchen counters to stools and tables in the home, these things are better left that way than to be used for storage, thereby causing disorganization in the home. They should be left clear so you can use them for their intended purposes, without having to clear them first. A dinner table is for eating meals, a kitchen counter for preparing food, a center table is meant to holding decorative ornaments, and a sideboard is for keys and other specific items.

Look, flat surfaces have a rule that should be religiously followed. Your kitchen counter top, the bathroom, floors, dining table, study table should not and must never have things on them unless they serve a purpose. There's no way around it. Having a dining table filled with books and things speaks volume about you as a person. It will reveal to any guest that you are clumsy and can't be trusted with important documents.

The clear surface rule is one of the best things ever to happen in the history of home organization. Seriously though, seeing junk on your table isn't the way to go. Even without the rule, you already know this, but you have decided to keep putting unnecessary things on your flat surfaces. I will give you the benefit of doubt, though. When you look through solutions I will give you throughout this book, you will do the right thing.

Now, let me tell you the flat surface rule: when it is a flat surface that includes the dining table, counter, floor you must never put something on it. Wait for it… it must stay clear of things unless that thing on the flat surface is a permanent fixture in the home.

You must wonder why you mustn't leave things on your flat surfaces (if they aren't permanent fixtures.) Well, the major reason you mustn't keep useless things on any flat surface of your home is because, the more you dump an important document (or anything) on your table (or any flat surface), the less you will stop. You will keep going, even when you start losing important things in your house.

It is normal to let yourself go and then the whole house becomes a mess, but do you really think letting your house look like a mad house is the best thing to put out there for people to see? Okay, let's forget about people for now. Do you think it is reasonable for you to arrange your books and 'neatly' pile them on the floor? Look, you will be prone to accidents if you are the type that puts your things on flat surfaces. Learn this now; it is very wrong.

When you keep putting useless things on a table or countertop or even a flat surface, you have this feeling of "what? It's not a big deal. It's just the table," but it is more than that. If you keep going, you won't even realize when your house turns into a mess. Then you become overly anxious and dread going to your own house. You become overwhelmed, and then you are forced to go through the strenuous process of actually cleaning your house. No, don't do that. Stop it. Stop making your house look like a junk place.

Let's talk about rule two for flat surfaces at home: You can always clear one flat surface at a time to make your work easy for you. Allow yourself to follow the method you want; the purpose is to make the surface neat. As you do it, you will become used to the idea of cleaning your flat surface and then you will likely not go back to what you used to do.

**One quick method that will help.** Do you want to see visible changes when it comes to flat surface arrangement? Try using a laundry basket then start with one room. Start putting things on the flat surface into your basket. Then try to put these things in the right place.

I know you are wondering, "But I don't have a place for some items?" Just create a place for these things. But please, let the place you have created not be a flat surface. Once you are done with a room, move to the next room and keep going until the flat surfaces in your room become free and clean.

If family comes for a visit and they dump things on your table, correct them. But the truth of the matter is, no one would ever be comfortable ruining a very neat, beautiful space.

Flat surfaces can be utilized as effective aesthetic improvements in your home. For example, a dining table could a dinner setting arrangement, with candles and flowers in the center. While improving the dining room's aesthetics, a permanent setting also helps reduce the temptation of placing random items there.

1. **The Dining Area**: The dining room is mostly an under-utilized area and sometimes over utilized area. When your dining area is underutilized, you probably only use it during special occasions, and when it is over utilized, you use it as a storage option. A dining area can be beautiful. To beautify your home, you can actually have a small dining area placed at the center of your home. It doesn't necessarily have to be extravagant. A simple dining table and chairs is enough to beautify a place. The awesome thing about a dining area is the fact that it can be decorated nicely and still have a comfortable vibe around it.

- You can emphasize the dining table with lights. If you get the idea of a minimalist design, then you will understand what I'm driving at. I discussed a minimalist design in the previous chapters, and I really think you should take it into consideration. The items on the dining table should always add to its appearance, not make it look ugly. One thing about any flat surface: less is more. If you decide to put into use this design style in your house, then the term less is more works very fine with dining areas. Be creative and let the imaginative juices flow.

• Flower vases, geometric designs, or anything that have to do with cutlery should only be found on the dining table.

• Anything you bring to your house must have its own place. Again, it shouldn't be on a flat surface, especially on the dining table.

• In order to avoid putting keys on your dining table, I advise you to create a place in the house for your keys. You fix up hooks behind the door and have keys hooked there instead of the dining table.

2. **Kitchen counter space**: A counter space is very important. You need it to prepare your food, not as a storage option. People make this mistake and forget how horrible the kitchen counters become when they leave their kitchen tools on it. So have your cabinet stacked up instead of on the counter; have your magnetic board ready for cutting tools, instead of placing them on the kitchen counter.

- Bonus point: it is better to have your cutlery stacked in an old mug and neatly put on the counter than to have your spoons and forks arranged on the counter.

- Keep a junk bowl.

- The vertical way of arranging stuff is the best option for you right now.

You see, when arranging the counter tops in my home, I prefer various sections to do my kitchen activities. Each time I use the kitchen, I want to be able to get things from the cabinet or cupboard easily. The truth is that the trick of categorizing items into different parts works. When I mentioned using the bin method in the bathroom cupboards, I meant it. Store some of your small kitchen stuff in it. Categorizing your kitchen utensils makes cooking easy. Do you love baking? Then find a spot for that on your counter space. Following this categorization keeps the kitchen orderly.

The way you design your kitchen counter space depends on the space left after the installation of cabinets and racks and even the layout of your kitchen. But no matter how much you keep trying to make your kitchen work, do you always end up looking for the spoon or the pot or the sachet of seasoning?

Most times, when I want to cook, I put everything I need next to me. Every ingredient, every kitchen utensil, every single thing is near. Just like me, you can always put some of these small items while cooking on a tray, so that way, you'll wash it and return everything to the right place. It doesn't necessarily have to be a tray though. Even a cutting board or a basket can be a great tool to place your ingredients.

You can store your beverages in a glass or plastic container. I use a transparent glass because it's easily obvious when it's dirty. In order to keep your kitchen counter clean and free, you need to find things around your home or find containers to keep your things.

The major reason you are reading this book is to learn what cleaning and organizing is all about. Then you should know that having a section where you store your cleaning tools is very important. I advise you create a station for every spot. This will keep the whole place from becoming a mess.

We all know the counter space is the most noticeable part of the kitchen, and it shouldn't be the part where you keep everything disorderly. For me, the counter space in my kitchen is more than just where I prepare my food. But with a lot of cooking functions to perform there, sometimes it might get a little difficult to keep up or put things in the right place. Finding what works for your counter space might be a challenge, but the more you read on, the more you get the drift where I'm heading with this.

3.     **Hallway Sideboards**: Normally, sideboards in the hallway are meant to serve as another surface along with the dining table. Hallway sideboards have performed various roles in the home, and I'm convinced they are a very important piece of furniture in the home. What is more beautiful about sideboards is the different ways they can be styled to fit the taste of the owner. They make a great additional aesthetics to the home. They can also be good in the bedroom and offices too, so don't limit its functions to the living room alone.

- When using a dresser in your bedroom, they can be a storage option. But the truth is that sideboards can be used next to the window or anywhere you think is deemed fit for your home. Sideboards are usually designed in a way that it has many drawers for anything you want to keep. Specifically, the number of drawers might sometimes depend on the size of the drawer. I mostly prefer storing my socks, undies and lady things in the sideboards in my bedroom, but putting your jeans, tops, gown in it might work too.

- On the other hand, the way you store things on and in the sideboard of a living room is different from the bedroom. But you must know that the sideboards in a living room can actual work in a number of ways. You can use it as a television stand, depending on the effect you are going for in your living room. The sideboard can also work for other electronics. What I love the most about sideboards is the vintage style it puts in the room it is placed.

- Hallways can look boring, but the moment you decide to add the touch of a sideboard to it, it gets transformed. Above your sideboard, you can place framed pictures of yourself or loved ones, but make sure you avoid too many pictures on there; you don't want it to look disorganized.

# CHAPTER SIX

# PROJECT ORGANIZATION

*"Better keep yourself clean and bright; you are the window through which you must see the world."*

According to InLoox, project organization is a process that provides the arrangement and decisions about the process and the realization of the project.

When it comes to organizing projects ahead of you, there are things you should always take into consideration: the cost of the project, when you plan to finish it, and the people you want involved. All these plans are what you will need to consider when you want to organize your house and keep it clean. To organize your home, I mentioned my first method of organization, which is removal. Removal involves taking out the storage solutions at home, repairing them if they are spoilt, or completely replacing them, because all these will determine the cost of the project. The stage where you start the removal process is when all your organization starts. When it comes to time lapse of your project, you need to take into consideration when you want your projects completed. Do you plan to make everything work and put in place in one week? Do you want to use one day for each room? You need to put this into consideration. Your time lapse for the project might also influence the cost of production; in fact, it'll determine your cost of production, depending on if you would be hiring someone to do most of the repairing and replacing. But remember, the more you know your way around a do-it-yourself project, the less money you spend. Last, you need to take into consideration if you'll get professionals in repair for this project you are about to embark on.

The basic thing is that planning things ahead might not wipe away the stress you might go through when organizing your home, but it'll lessen the stress. But then, a disorganized home brings stress.

An organized environment is calming. Being in a place categorized by direction, serenity, and a vivid expression of your perceptions can also aid in relaxing the nerves and aid in freeing anxiety. There is a sense of peace in organized homes, and that is one of the basic things you need. Returning from work or anywhere to a well-organized home can really improve your life because you will always have this air of calmness surrounding you. It will make you feel like you've just stepped into a refuge far from the stress in the real world outside.

All in all, a disorganized, chaotic home can give you problems far more than just anxiety. If you can't call anywhere your safe place, somewhere you can sleep, bathe, put your belongings and know where to find them again, then it is a problem.

In fact, there is a Chinese discipline named Feng Shui that says a properly organized house brings good things in life. But generally, who doesn't enjoy a calm environment? So, how then do you achieve that serenity if you do not plan your organization project ahead of time? No matter how much time you are to spend organizing your home, it can be a hard task. Starting the project can be difficult but running your project smoothly until the end can be a lot harder.

Sincerely, I have been stressed about organizing my home before discovering the hacks to do it right. If you want to get it right, just like me, then I'll show you all it takes. Practice makes perfect. Planning something can get you a productive result and get you to achieve it in a less stressful manner. It can be exciting most times to start and organize your whole house right away though. You already think you have everything figured out, so you rush into the organization without thinking of where to store one item or the other. Other times, you store some items and then two weeks after, you're looking for the same items, thinking it got lost. The reality is that, if you had planned out your project normally, you wouldn't be in this mess.

So stop now!

This is not a road you want to follow without proper planning. You don't want to risk misplacing your things all in the name of fixing up your house.

Start making plans as early as possible. A good plan will birth good management skills and good management is what will push you to successful organization.

To make things work, view a broader picture in your mind and imagine how you would want your house to be. You know why you have to plan ahead and visualize what you really want. you know why you need to identify your goal and why you need to create timing for your project. All these things mentioned are what project organization encompasses. There is no doubt that planning will slow down the project at first, but sincerely, it will save you a lot of time and stress. Planning your home organization can be invaluable.

Do not confuse project organization to making a list of dates and all. In other words, making a schedule all boils down to project organization. You need to set everything in motion right now, create the steps, and get your house organized.

**Why you must have a project plan for organizing your home**.

This stage of organizing your home comes before any other thing in the list of things you plan to do. In fact, without this stage, I believe you won't even have a list of things you want to remove, repair, and replace. It is after this stage that every other stage will be carried out to achieve your final goal, which is to organize your home neatly and always keep it clean.

One of the qualities of a brilliant plan is for you not to fear whatever issues are to come once your home organization is set in motion. I'm certain you are reading this book right now because you do not have the experience to get your house in order, so here are ways to plan ahead when organizing your home.

**Plan your home organization ahead of time**

Most home decorators plan rearrangement of the home they want to work on ahead of time, and you should too. It may take some hours of the day, and it might only take two to three days, but it'll pay off sooner or later. The major goal is to define your plan for organizing your home because it will save you a lot of time, money, and stress.

For you to be able to organize your project properly ahead of time, I need you to be able to use the following tactics:

Identify what you want to begin with: Do you want to begin with your kitchen or living room or the garage? Understanding the basics will help you get ahead with your project. But the truth of the matter is, even if you claim you want to organize your home and keep it clean, it wouldn't achieve anything, so start something now. Plan ahead and stick to your project plans.

Have you set an objective? Like I mentioned, to clean up your house and have everything in order isn't just about saying it but about the goal you have for the project. Picture your house in your head then think of how you want it to turn out. What you imagine and wish for is what your end goal should be. Do you want to maintain a playful outlook in your home? Do you want a minimalist appearance? Just think, and if it'd help you, then search on Pinterest. So what do you want to achieve? I'm guessing it's to have a beautiful apartment while maintaining order and cleanliness.

So, define your goal now. That is what will help you get your house in order.

If you'll get people to work it out for you, then you need to plan now.

Set a deadline now. Achieving a task isn't something that can be completed at one time. You can't just decide to organize your home today and then do it immediately. There has to be a process to follow, and if you will follow a process, then create a deadline. Determining how long your task will take will help you to keep your head on track and finish your project.

Ask people for ideas. Ask what they think. Get a friend to look through your plan, specifically a friend who has an eye for good things. This way, you will be able to tweak their ideas with yours. Another thing I look out for is to make my plan for my home organization as flexible as possible so that changing some things won't become a difficult task. The moment your plan is set and your friend also brings a great plan for you, it'll work as a major road plan to getting your dream home. Therefore, plan, organize, identify your goal, and get feedback.

Set your project on the right path. I can never over emphasize how much I believe in planning. No matter how much you think it's not necessary, it'll always be necessary. To make sure you get your home items in order just the way you've imagined your house to be, start making schedules. It shouldn't take many days, and you want to keep maintaining your clean and orderly home, so you need to keep going back to rearrange when things get disorderly.

Another crucial step is for you to believe in yourself to make the right choice. No matter how much you get feedback, even if your friend thinks your idea was great, if you don't believe in your guts, you'll end up making your house into a huger mess.

**How long should it take to finish your home organization?**

If you plan well, then you won't have a problem with time. My favourite method of estimating the time I'll take to finish arranging my house is to set out a plan. So plan, plan and plan.

**Ways to maintain your project to the end**

When it comes to maintaining a plan for home organization, you are allowed to remove and add things to the items you intend to change. You want to repair something? Then do that. If you want to replace, you are free to do that too. These things will set your project in motion and keep you maintaining it.

It is better you begin organizing a single room, a selection of rooms, or your entire house; allocate a table, a lounge or perhaps a bed, as a temporary place where you can empty boxes, cupboards and drawers. This will allow you to see duplicates, items that you want to sell and those items that should be stored together.

Allocate a realistic amount of time to complete the reorganization, so you can finish fully. It is better to complete one or two tasks in a day than have nine or ten incomplete.

This is also an opportunity to label bins and boxes, so you know what is inside them later. Labeling also makes for quickly storing new items in an allocated location.

**How do you really plan to make this work?**

I took you through a brief process of project organization, but I want us to go deeper and see the practical ways you can actually organize your things before taking action.

Start with any part of the home. I will pick the kitchen as an example.

Food preparation section: What is done in that section? What tools are used in that section? Cutting tools, mixing bowls, measuring cups, seasoning cubes are used during food preparation. Now, I'm not asking you to store your seasoning ingredients in the same place as your mixing bowl. I'm telling you to focus on that section and find a way to organize these items in the same space.

**Cooking:** Pots and pans should actually be kept in the same space.

**Dish washing and storage**: I am of the opinion that putting a plate rack filled with plates is better off next to the sink. You get what I mean, right?

**Storage**: You know the canned food lying on your counter tops? Well, do something about it too. Keep these canned foods, bottled products in a place.

Remember I said something about keeping products that perform similar functions in a side in the drawer? Well, this is one moment you need to follow those tips. Pick each part of your house, find the items that perform a similar function and start organizing on your notes until you are done.

# CHAPTER SEVEN

# ACCESSIBILITY

*"Cleanliness and order are not matter of instinct; they are matters of education, and like most great things, you must cultivate a taste for them."* -Benjamin Disraeli

Keeping your house in order is very important; there is no doubt about it. What is more interesting about keeping your house nice and clean is the result you get. Can you picture the outlook already? Yes, clean, neatly arranged books on the top shelf, home tools stored in the farthest part of the shelves in the garage and on and on. Wait, stop right there. I know you've followed my advice right from the beginning of this book, but have you seen anything about accessibility? I'm guessing you are thinking no. You are right. But it is very important for you to keep that in mind when trying to keep your house organized. You should always be conscious of your accessibility to the things you stored. If you keep a tool you constantly use in a place that isn't accessible, I promise you will end up getting your whole house disorganized. You will pull things apart just to get that one thing you didn't store reasonably.

When I mentioned you putting your tools in the top shelf of the room, I don't mean it's bad, but do you know how to get your things from that top shelf? Do you even have a ladder? I know your answer is no too, so why the hell would you store your things up there far away from your grasp?

It is only normal for you to make sure that regularly used things in each room are the easiest to access. You shouldn't need to bend down too far to get to commonly used items nor should you require a ladder. Items used infrequently could be stored higher (thereby needing a ladder) or in secluded storage areas that need more time and effort to access.

Small internal ladders or the ones that can be folded under the steps, so that it would also be stored where they are easily accessible, are great but be careful as these can be trip hazards. Storage locations also need to have enough space in front of them for you to stand and remove or place items. You may also need space to pivot and leave that area.

We've established how important it is to organize your home. I have mentioned organizing every room in your house from the garage to your bedroom, but now it's time to know how to arrange these things in a way that makes it accessible for you without needing to get a ladder. Even if you might need a ladder from time to time, you should keep it to a minimum, and if you will keep at a minimum, you need to follow the rules of storage.

There are times your house has ended up being a mess, so you decide to tidy up your space from your closet, to your room to your living room, to your kitchen, to your garage. You know what is really funny is that I used to have issues with so many things in my home, especially when it came to saving mail. It always ended becoming a mess in the house. Do you know where this is going?

So in this chapter, we will go deeply into what organization is all about and the exact ways to do it. Ways to do it that won't make things go missing at the end of the day. The previous chapters show you how to apply my approaches by removing, assessing, planning, and putting these methods into good use. Do not start work without reading the previous chapters and really understanding what the tips are meant for. The previous chapters serve as a foundation but what you do with this chapter is what will catapult your home into a beautiful abode where you want it to be. So sit down, read, and understand what I'm about to teach you.

**Where do you begin?**

If you have a disorganized home, it can be overwhelming to know where to start. My advice for you is to pick a place. Remember, in the previous chapter, I hammered on the removal of storage solutions you do not need. It is very important for you to do that. So, pick a place in your home; preferably, you can choose somewhere in your home where you spend most of your time. The truth is that the spot where you use the most is where you achieve most of your things, isn't that so? If the spot where you achieve most of your goals is a mess, then you will have a big problem.

In fact, I give it to you now. Do not bother picking a spot. I advise you to pick your favourite spot of the house and start from there. Having a favourite room of your house all depends on your interest as a person. If you are a makeup artist, then your room might be your favourite spot to do your work. If you are a photographer, then maybe anywhere in your home might be your favourite spot, but I believe you get my drift, right?

**Start from somewhere. Don't start big.**

You organized a lot of times, but I can bet you've never done it like I'm about to teach you. This whole process will be new to you, but if you follow a small by small step process, then you will cover a whole range of things. So again, remove, assess, and work things out. This is one of the biggest points of an actual organizer. If you employ one, they will start small too, so follow that lead and do the same for yourself. It makes your work very easy.

Yes, your house isn't organized. Your books, your clothing, your compact disks, your shoes are everywhere. You know you are supposed to gather it and put it in their right place, but the truth of the matter is that you never had a spot for it in the first place. It has always been all over the place. But like I have said and would always insist on, you cannot organize your house all at once. Choose the place in your house you'd like to rearrange and completely organize it before moving on to another one. Little by little, put thing here where it is neat and there where it is organized, and voila you have your place set up. Have this at the back of your mind though; disorganizing your house didn't start in one day. It is because you didn't pay attention, and that is why you assumed it just started like boom! My house is a huge mess. Nope. Same way organization should work. You shouldn't ever assume it is something you can do at once.

Oh, I get it. You are questioning yourself like: "How the hell does she even know this?"

I know these things about a disorganized home because, just like you, I have had problems with a disorganized home when I was younger, but I stopped and told myself it was time to get things right.

There are many people who have dished out tips that organization can take a whole year. I watched a video like that where the tips were dished out, and I wondered why you would take so long to organize your things. No, that is a big lie. I do not think you should take eternity to have your house organized. I believe you want to take two weeks or three weeks, and the good news is that the time you use in planning isn't part of the weeks. So this means good planning equals good outcome of organization. Do not try to finish one aspect in an hour or two. A day or two is fine for each project you set out to do. The goal is to do it right while setting a time limit for it. Take for example, if you have six weeks for organizing your home and you probably have a job that takes a lot of time from you, check below and use this method to set up your space.

Week one = your room (closet, shoes, work table etc.)

Week two = your bathroom

Week three = your hallway

Week four = your living room

Week five = kitchen

Week six = garage

Okay, six weeks is good if you are a busy bee. If you are not, then one week or two is enough for you to make everything work.

Start getting together everything you will need. But the thing is that, if you've read and absorbed the first few chapters, you will know things to gather for your storage solutions. Gathering these things will keep you focused on the work ahead.

**These are the supplies you will need to kickstart this project**:

Container

Shelf

Boxes

Drawers etc.

**1.    What will you do with the bedroom?** Now, let's assess your bedroom again, but I need you to answer this; do you work from home? If you do, that aspect will be discussed in the process of this part of the book. Remember the point of this section is not only to teach you to store your things, but to keep it in ways that will give you easy accessibility.

**Why would you like to get your home organized?**

- You want a neat house.

- You want to have a stress free house.

- You want a sense of serenity.

What is the major cause of your disorganized bedroom?

**Insufficient storage**: Your bedroom can serve a purpose. It can be a studio for a photographer, for a makeup artist, an office for a full time writer. Right now, the solution isn't to know what you will throw away; you already followed the removal step. You've already set your goal, so the best thing now is to find more storage solutions for your things. Determine what activities you do most in your room. I will help you with ideas that will help you determine how you should store your things according to the interests and activities you perform in your room. Below, I will classify storage tips and easy ones that will give you accessibility to your things.

- **Sleeping**

Items used for sleeping: Blankets, Pillows, Eye mask, Night gowns, Pajamas.

Storage solutions: To store these items that will give you easy accessibility, you need to neatly fold some on your bed, and some in drawers. But mostly, your bedside or bed is the best storage method.

- **Reading**

Items used when reading: Books, magazines, newspapers etc.

Storage solutions: To store your items in the easiest ways, put it in a bedside table, neatly. Just make sure you keep it is neat, and if you have a shelf, then it's even better.

- **Priming**

Items used when priming: jewelry, cosmetics, tweezers, hairbrushes etc.

Storage solutions: Get a vanity dresser. Keep makeup brushes in a container. The basic point is that you should just put these things in the right place. You don't want to use your body cream and then start looking for it everywhere just because you put it on your bed or bedside table and forgot it was there. That is the purpose of your vanity table, for priming.

- **Writing**

Items used for writing: Pens, paper, laptop, notebooks etc.

Storage solutions: You can either have a table by the window to put these things or put it by your bedside. But make sure you have a container for stationary, provided you have a lot of it.

Now that has been settled, make sure you do not forget the furniture in your room. If you are an avid reader or a writer, try to work with what you love doing and keep the necessary things you use by your bedside table.

Do you like to see your vanity dresser first or a mirror? Then arrange it that way. Just keep in mind the major thing you need to get right is to make sure it is accessible.

Do you need ideas to make your room larger and make it appear organized? Follow these tips. More space, more accessibility. This simply means a more spacious place will give room to access to your things easily. You can keep your extra blanket, bed cover and pillow case under your bed. In fact, it is a brilliant idea because, when you need to lay in your bed, that's the first thing you will think about. Accessibility! Keep that in mind.

Get a bedside table that you can also store things in. For example, a bedside table with drawers. That way, you can keep your writing stuff as a writer and still neatly arrange your books on it.

Let your closet work for you. There are other closets that can be your house. In fact, it is advisable to have these storage solutions, because it is what makes your home organized. Go to your room now and assess the number of closets you have. Then start assigning the closets to everything you want to store. This storage solution can be changed. Sometimes, you might have so many books that even a bedside table won't contain it. A shelf in your bedroom can work or you can just put your to-be-read books next to you on your bedside. Make things work with these ideas.

**Reasons you should get your closet in order:**

- To improve your closet.

- To be able to find what you need when you look for it.

- To be able to make more room for more clothes. An arranged space will create more space.

- Easy access to clothes.

2. **Get your Kitchen together**: The kitchen is more than just for cooking. And as you read, you will find out ways to store your things, remember where you keep them, and get easy access.

**Canned products**

Items that fall into this category: bottles, canned foods, sachet products etc.

How to get easy access to it: Jelly cupboards at neck level.

**Preparation of food**

Items that fall into this category: Bowls for mixing, seasoning, blenders, juicer, measuring cans, spoons, knives, cutting boards.

How to get easy access to it: You can keep these things in the cabinet above and the ones below.

**Dishes**

Items that fall into this category: Normal dishes, glasses, mugs, bowls

How to get easy access to it: You can keep it in the cabinet above the sink, but I have a thing against putting your dishes up there because I can't imagine myself stressing to get a plate I use every day, and I don't feel it's reasonable for you to stress yourself either. My advice for you is to put your glass cups and bowls there. Get a nice double decker plate rack that would have a space for mugs on the second layer. Some racks even come with a compartment where spoons can be kept.

3.     How much time you spend in your living room doesn't matter. Even if you spend less time, you should still take care of your living

room. If you take care of your living room, put it in mind that you need to put it in order in a way the items are accessible. How do you do that? But before we go further, let me tell you the benefits of keeping your living room organized and accessible.

**Reasons you need to organize your living room**

- The living room is a place to spend time with friends and family members. To receive visitors normally.

- To be able to bring visitors without being scared.

Why your living room is always disorganized and why you can't get access to it:

- Your things do not have somewhere to be kept. This is plain and simple. So, let's get down to business. How do you arrange your living room and still get easy access to it?

**Reading books**

Items that can be used for reading:

- Magazines, books, pens etc.

**Storage ideas that will give you access to your reading items**:

- Bookshelves are the best way to store books in the living room. And to avoid losing your books, you can keep them by colours or genres. Those methods are the best ways.

When it comes to organization, I believe you already know how important it is to get your things accessible. One problem people who are new with organization usually have is that they confuse clean with organized. But it goes deeper than that.

A clean environment is just what you see on the surface, but an organized surrounding takes a lot of effort. Cleanliness is just what the name is, but organization encompasses a clean, sparkling environment and well-arranged household items.

What then are the causes of the mess in your home? What are the problems you will face when you confuse a clean house with an organized one?

**Error one**: Mixing up the meaning of clean and organized

I have made mistakes of arranging a bunch of books and newspapers on the center table of my living room. Believe me when I say it looked clean, but it didn't mean I was organized.

If I needed a particular book, I'd have to scatter the books just to find what I needed. It wouldn't happen if I had a shelf where I arranged my books according to colours or genre. So before you bring new things to your home, you have to create a spot for storing them while keeping in mind if it'd ever be easily accessible. Once you understand this process, your 'organized books on the table' will vanish.

**Error two**: Is it really wise to make the counter completely clear?

When you have taken every object from the counter top in your kitchen, make sure you try as much as possible to leave behind the ones you use on a daily basis. If you love making soup or smoothies, then you need to find a spot for your blender. Things are easier to be maintained in the house when you have the things you need accessible or at hand. All items in your home, whether kitchen or not, should have a designated spot.

**Error three**: Stacking too much on the refrigerator

I cringe whenever I watch movies with the refrigerator stacked with different magnets, notes, letters and photos. It is plain messy, and even though you think it is easily "accessible," it's not a good look for your house. In the course of this book, I made sure it will take you through the process of keeping small stuff, especially important papers. Have you ever tried using a clipboard that would be hung on the kitchen wall. You can then pin notes, lists, reminders etc. on the clipboard. Once your clipboard is full, then it's time to find some boxes or so to keep them neat. Remember, accessibility matters. Besides, you might end up not needing the notes because sometimes no one reads them.

**Error four**: Disorganized Kitchen counter

So you just finished your plates and you decided the best place to keep it is to 'neatly' put it over each one on the counter top. Look, we get it; your kitchen counter sparkles from cleanliness and your plates too, but this just proves the point of organization. They're a different ball game. Get a plate rack, fix it up, and arrange the plates in an organized manner.

**Error five**: You have the kitchen packed with cabinets

The journey of organization is not easy, and one of its biggest problems is making decisions on what to keep and let go of. But that is not just what I'm trying to get to. You see, when you keep kitchen cabinets because you want to store your things, you'll end up forgetting which cabinet contains the item. Accessibility becomes difficult due to your inability to keep track in the kitchen.

**Error six**: Deserting by-the-door paper storage

I have mentioned this from the beginning, the middle, and the end. It's so important for you to give a home to every item in your house. Paperwork, files, receipts etc. should all have a place they can be kept. A crate, shoe box etc. will work fine for storing paperwork. You wouldn't want to lose your thing because you've been disorganized. Looking for these things when you need it most can be difficult unless you have a home for it.

**Error seven**: Clothing problems

Most women would be glad to have a walk-in-closet, but you think about what you make use of before using all that space for a bunch of shoes. If you are not wearing all the shoes all the time, then don't you think you should find a space for new ones you wear on a daily basis.

If you are the type that exercises, then you should have your running shoes and clothes If you go running every day, those shoes should be in the front. If you have boots, and you don't wear them on a daily basis then its time you keep them away and arrange your work (or school) shoes closer. You need to face reality with items that are worn every day.

**Error eight**: Drawers and stuff

Just shoving your stuff in boxes and drawers will never make your home organized. Yes, they are great for keeping things, but it only works well when you arrange your things by compartments or use dividers in drawers. Besides, if you just throw your things aimlessly into the drawer, you will always find it difficult to find things you need.

**Error nine:** Stop with the storage bins

Having too many storage bins can cause a mess in your home. Instead of stacking your house here and there with storage bins, why not look for the ones you have at home?

Buying so many storage solutions is one error people make when it comes to home organization. A lot of people think bringing home a bunch of storage containers, drawers, and cabinets will solve their organization problem, but it will just become more of a problem. You'll lose track of where you keep some of your things. I'm guessing you won't want that.

You can also try putting shoe boxes inside your drawer to have your things arranged neatly.

**Error ten**: Use labels

It's good if you have storage containers, boxes, and mason jars, but you need to know what each container actually contains. You don't want to put your earrings in a container meant for paper clips just because you forgot to do the needful. That's when the importance of labeling pops up. You get to take a purse when you are about to throw an item in a wrong container.

**Error eleven**: Family photos are lovely, but too much is bad.

I know someone who puts up different pictures on the wall because she doesn't have a good place to keep them. I'll advise you to get a photo album and keep the pictures in there, and then look for a way to build a gallery wall; you can use the space on the wall that leads up the stairs.

**Error twelve**: Letting the cords become a mess

One of the few things I have real issues with is wires on the walls and floors. If left without any form of arrangement, they end up becoming a problem, especially when it's time to vacuum the living room. Having cables on the wall and floor of any part of the home is a total mess. Make use of paper clips, foam boards, or a shoe box to create a beautiful design that will keep your wires intact without any disturbance. You can easily pick your iPhone charger among other chargers because you've done the right thing by arranging the cords.

**Error thirteen**: Book shelves are good only when they are arranged.

Having a book shelf is pretty awesome, but it all boils down to how they are styled. Making sure your books follow a colour code or genre is a sure way to find a book to read easily.

**Error thirteen**: All books don't have to be in the open

Letting the books you love or admire sit on the shelf is the surest way to find the book to read easily. If you put every book you own on the shelf, believe me you'll end up hating your shelf and books, which is something you do not want. Remember, the key here is to keep accessibility in mind when organizing your home.

# CHAPTER EIGHT

# STORAGE VOLUME

*"What separates two people most profoundly is a different sense and degree of cleanliness."* -Friedrich Nietzsche

It is important to limit the amount of storage you have available in the home. You need to be able to live in each room and not be subservient to your possessions and storage. Movement from room to room needs to be efficient and smooth, which promotes satisfied living. Too much storage can disrupt the enjoyment of your home, in a similar way that having a cluttered home or too many possessions can.

Surplus available storage may also promote purchasing items in order to fill the space – items that you don't really need or want. Available storage space does not require that it be filled. When planning on purchasing and installing storage solutions, try to find a balance between space utilization now and what you might require in the future.

Arranging a room is difficult to an extent, and it is even more difficult to fill up a space without making it look like a mess. How do you do it? How can one arrange a big room and still not leave too much space? I need you to do something for me in this part of the book. I want you to pay close attention to this chapter. The problem with organizing your home is that you might end up making too much space, and it makes it feel like you don't have stuff in your house. You don't want to invite someone to your house and make them feel that way.

Your house is meant to be comfy, a common ground for talking to visitors and your family, and relaxing by reading books and watching movies. The mistake you will make is to make it feel like a stage in a theater where you perform for the audience. First, take a huge breath, close your eyes, and picture a stage where dramas are performed: you see bright lights and an open space… too much space. Yes, that's right. Would you want your room to be that blank just like a stage? A home is supposed to feel homey, neat, organized with a beautiful theme that portrays a home!

I always say this and it is true: When you have a place and it has few items occupying it, then it's a waste of air. You know the vibe your house gives when you do not have enough items covering the floor space? A minimalist house with no household items. Yes, I have been raving about the minimalist approach in the house, but they have their own disadvantages, even though it makes the house neat and organized.

Yes, when you follow the minimalist process in your house, you will learn to keep things put away; you hardly get attached to an item at home because you believe these items will make your house dirty.

Your house will look sharper with good light reflecting inside and make you feel like it's paradise. But then when you throw out all these things in your house, there will be a time you would pause and wonder what you should put in your kitchen or living room or bedroom. The minimalist approach in your house gives you air and space for almost any home activity. You have a feel of being structured, and that makes you so proud, but getting rid of things, especially things you need, just because you want to portray a neat spacious house will be mentally draining.

You begin to spend more money for a structurally neat space while creating unnecessary spaces that can be utilized. You become afraid to buy new things, and when you do, it will be the same structured item that can still make your house look too spacious. It is good to have a neat and spacious environment, but in all, you should put enough things in your house too. The major determinants of making your house look 'too spacious' are colour, furniture, texture and volume of household items.

To use enough storage space in your living room, here's how to do it right.

### 1. Furniture

Do you realize small objects in a large place make it look big? Imagine, throwing a needle in a bag of sand and expecting to find it. You can't find it. There is no way around it, and that's the same with small furniture in a large room. A chair as small as a baby's cradle in a large living room will look awkward. In fact, it will never look beautiful. Remember when I said, aesthetics matters when it comes to organization and making your things look neat at home. In order to work your things beautifully in a large room, all the items you put in it should work well with the space.

To get started with the large living room, you need to place long sofas and elaborate arm chairs with throw pillows. You can try a large center rug on the floor, and a beautiful, elaborately designed center table. How about a nice study section in the living room? All in all, make sure you follow a nice design pattern. The point is to make sure the room doesn't look too big with too few properties and too filled up with your home items.

If you have enough money to spend, then get furniture fixed on the wall in your living room. If you don't want furniture, how about you try a wall painting, but go for the big ones with a hint of vintage.

Try a shelf stuffed with books. Make it look like a library, but mind you, these ideas only works if you are willing to spend cash. Mix up your shelf with cabinets and drawers. Furniture like this will buff up your living room in a classy, beautiful way. Consider adding something you really care about to a corner in your living room.

## 2. Rearrange

One of the best methods a home decorator uses when designing a large room is to make it into different rooms. Such rooms can serve as the bedroom, kitchen, or even a photo studio. These kinds of apartments are suitable for people living in high-rise buildings and can only get a one room apartment.

If it's a rather large room, then you've got tricks to play with. Are you a writer living in such an apartment and you are looking for ways to make it look... less empty? Try creating a living out of your space and add a few living room features to it; create a kitchen from in there and start arranging. If you've got all your kitchen items, then start arranging it just like I mentioned in the previous chapters. The point is to be in-between this time around. Not too big of a living room and not too cramped.

Do you work from home and you've being dying to have an office? Then I think it's time you get your working table and chair next to your window. If you categorize your furniture, let it show it performs different functions but neatly do this. Try dividing the space into manageable but spacey kind of chunks. This works well for any type of woman: art lover, writer, photographer, makeup artist etc. Even if you have no interest in art, it'll still work greatly for you.

Try placing your long sofa in the living room. You can try different angles. Sometimes, angles are what you need for your room to work.

I find that arranging your sofas, whether long or portable, around the television will bulk things up.

Have a moveable desk place in the next room, and let it serve as a kitchen. I'll suggest you keep the kitchen a little bit farther down the big living room. You will especially need to fix a bunch of cabinets on the wall or a utensil storage solution.

As you read and think of what your room will look like with these ideas teaching you how to make your room less spacious, I trust you are truly thinking of ways to do your homework. Picturing your one room apartment divided into sections that serve a purpose will not only help your taste of design, it will also improve its beauty.

## 3. Painting

There are many tricks when it comes to using colours. Colours can change the outlook of a place with simple tricks, and for a long time, home decorators have learned these tricks, and so far, it has worked fine for them.

For a room to appear larger, you need to go for colours at the end of the wheel. This trick is useful, and you wouldn't know if you have never tried it.

You can also make the floor in your house dark and the walls light. This contrast will make the floor space very large, creating an illusion.

When you have a low ceiling, changing the colour to a light one will make it look large.

When you choose a furniture that is the same colour as the walls, the room is bound to look bigger while making the furniture small.

Now, you must wonder why I mentioned the above if all you need to learn is how to the home space properly. Well, if these tricks make your room look larger, then the opposite will make it look smaller.

White rooms look too big in my eyes. When I was younger, I used to think it was my imagination, but when I went deeper into housing designs, I learned colours truly matter. When the colour of your room is bright, it brings more illumination and causes it to look bigger.

Don't go thinking: "I'll shut my room from natural light." Trust me, it'll be pretty stupid. But your goal is to make your living room look filled up.

Yes, it's purely obvious. Without someone telling you, I'm guessing you know that colours trim sizes down. Wear black if you want to look slim; that's what fashion experts say. As a room expert, I'm telling you this now. A darker living room will not only make your living room smaller, but it'll make it look cozy. When you have a less reflective painting plastered on your wall, floor or ceiling, it gives a vibe of a house nicely organized yet less spacious.

To avoid staying in a large apartment after numerous rearrangement with nothing changing for the better, I advise you to opt for new paint. Revamp your home. Plaster up some deep colours and avoid white, baby pink, cream, lavender and go for deep gray and dark brown paints. It will work, I promise, and you'll love it.

All in all, though, what matters isn't only about filling up your living room. You could as well go for something light or in between if that's what you like.

**4. Textures and pattern**

I love gritty and spiky textures. It's usually beautiful, but what I like isn't what I'm here to tell you. What you want matters a lot. When I mentioned going for an over the top furniture, I didn't mean it only had to be a furniture. It could as well work with what is on your wall.

Going for big patterns with extravagant designs on a wall will make it seem less spacious. What's more powerful are nice curtains with dark colours. These dark coloured curtains will work beautifully well when they are up on bright coloured walls. If you want to have an even more dramatic look, then curtains with large patterns are great.

A nice wallpaper with beautiful dark designs works too just don't go for something flowery since the point of this section is to teach you how to use your home space and still keep your house organized.

A nice wooden wall works well, especially when it's painted deep brown like a coffee colour. Do not use lacquered wood. It is advisable to try out painted woods. If you are going to use metals in the house as an option, then go for dull metals like wrought iron. Shiny walls aren't a great idea. Glass or mirrored ones aren't advisable either. Do you know how white houses with glass doors always look way bigger than they should?

From outside, a house decorated with dark stones and dark wooden materials always looks great. Do you picture how beautiful it'll be? Try out these tips and fill up your empty rooms at home.

# CHAPTER NINE

# THE SMALL STUFF

*"Quality, service, cleanliness and value."*-Steve Ross

Although the procedure of arranging small writing materials and other writing objects is pretty easy, sometimes it might not be evident where you want to store your writing materials that are excessively all over your writing table and somewhere else. Okay, I know you have been waiting for ways you can store your writing materials at home. I am really excited to show you the way out because even I had an issue with that a long time ago. I love reading. My reading habits are pretty vast, and when I do, I love writing down the small stuff that connects with me in a write up. So, yes, this part of the book is as important as every part because, somehow, you keep wondering if keeping the small stuff in your house is actual junk, but it is not. This chapter will assist you when it comes to some concepts that will get you on the right path with various resourceful rearrangements.

1.  Start the process by checking out your stationery and choose the storage ideas that will work best for you. Well, except if you have magical powers and if you do not have so much stationery at home, you can't get this done in minutes. But the truth of the matter is that, this part encompasses all the small stuff in your house. Fix adequate time. You are probably thinking, "I'm a busy bee. I don't have the

time." Relax, it won't kill you if you use the weekend you are supposed to hang out to arrange your things at home. Take, for example, when you have a break in the afternoon even before going to school or work and during your day off. These all will be dependent on the part of the house you want to organize. Also, gather supplies you will need from around the home or that you have purchased.

2.      You can take a Saturday and start with small stuff. How about before heading to school? I don't know what time you head to work, but if you don't go early, then take your time and arrange your small stuff. You can use your day off and start arranging.

3.      Let's start by taking out your stationery and see where it will fit when it comes to storage. Remember, we are not throwing things out or decluttering anything. The point of this is to know sections where to store your stationery.

4.      Find storage solutions that aren't expensive in a dollar store, stationery store, and other stores that sell cute storage solutions. You can try these stores during sale time. So, start gathering your supplies: containers, rubber bands, and other supplies you will need to store things at home.

5.      Find different containers for storage in your house. Seriously, I tried some cute cat-like designs using a bottle of soda at home. But all these depend on what you are going for. This especially works well for someone with a playful personality or the theme you are going for.

If you are looking into spicing up your room, then you can search do-it-yourself revamping room ideas. Anyway, get your containers ready. You can make containers from the least expected objects, so open your mind to new ideas. Have you checked out if you have some containers in your cabinets, garage/store or bathrooms? Then maybe they might come in useful for storage solutions for your stationery. My point is that, even if you don't have these things at home, try as much as possible to buy some containers, label them, and hop to the next stage of storing your stationery. Keep your pencils separate from your pens, rubber bands, erasers, and every other writing material you have.

6.     Be artistic. Try to switch the normal to something cute or beautiful. When you do this yourself, people will realize it's not something they've seen anywhere. Look for any size of box, although an average size works fine. Whether wooden or cardboard will work just fine with what you are about to do. Put recycled paper on the top of the box. The next thing is for you to colour the lid and the box. Be watchful of the material though; sometimes, some paints don't suit the materials of the container. Wait for it to dry. Depending on the paint and material, drying the paint might take a day. But if you want something quicker, try putting it under the sun. Be careful not to get it destroyed by rain though. Once you have it dried, then you should put some cardboard in the box. This method can be a bit tricky, but the goal is to have sections in the box. Try using glue to keep the

cardboard in place. When the glue is dry, you can put some paperclips in it and many other writing and reading materials.

7. Mason jars are a woman's best friend. Like for real, they are. If you have some mason jars at home, then it makes your work easier. The vibe in your room will be chic, cute and beautiful. If you work from home, it can work fine on your study table, giving your study section a less stiff vibe. Which is great, right? If you love colourful and playful colours then try painting the jar or add a little glitter. It won't hurt.

8. Have you ever tried tackles boxes? They can be a little pricey, and I won't blame you if you think putting money out there is too much, but having a home for the small stuff in your house matters. If it's urgent for you to decorate your house and you've got no money then go with containers you have at home. If you have extra cash, you can buy it. If you have little cash to spend and you are not in a hurry, then wait for sales.

9. You should try shoe boxes for your supplies. Try something fantastic. Let your creativity flow.

Now, let's get back to arranging your bills, receipts, and other important papers. Yes, I know your drawer is full of these documents. These things should be sorted out now. You are tired of the way it scatters all around your home. Maybe one time you need to back date through a document of five months ago, but because you've never arranged them, you can't find it. So far, if all the questions up there were answered with yes, and then let's get started.

**Start with categorizing**

Yes, separate your bills, receipts, and documents accordingly.

This separation process involves two procedures. The first is to find a temporary storage solution so that you can keep these documents somewhere. So put them together first in a temporary place. I advise you to sort each document, arrange them, band them with rubber bands, and let the method continue until you band each type of document differently. Your telephone bills should be placed differently with a rubber band and other documents should too. Once done, put them together in a place; a shoe box will work excellently for this storage method. Since everything is tied together separately with rubber, you can easily find documents you received even years back.

A lot of people usually stock their drawers with documents but don't be that person. This will result in a lot of mess.

The second procedure is to store your other documents in another box. These documents can include the ones you use for your day to day shopping. The ones you got from a grocery store and some you might need to remember the price of a product. Don't forget accessibility is important in all these things. The thing is that, if you need a receipt that contains groceries and it is with a pile of other documents, you'll have problem getting things you need.

I'm hoping you understand what I'm getting at. One box to store away things you don't use every time and the other box to store your day to day documents.

Put the documents in a temporary storage in an organized section. If you've followed every step I put down, these things will come easy. If you are into jobs that usually include a lot of files, you can even arrange them in alphabetical order, the most important documents and according to colours. Try to make these arrangements constantly. The first Sunday of each month or last Saturday of every month can work perfectly fine.

**Here are a number of documents you can sort out in your home**:

1. **Tax documents**: Taxation documents usually include receipts, bank statements, tax return documents etc.

2. **Insurance document:** They include life insurance documents, health insurance documents, vehicle insurance documents etc.

3. **Banking documents:** They include your bank statements and your credit card documents or literature.

4. **Investment documents:** Stock documents, mutual fund documents etc.

5. Loan documents

6. Medical records

7. Home appliances

8. Personal

You should keep documents online, offline, and in hard copy form, provided there is a significance of every document. The period in which you preserve these documents is vital as far as you won't discard significant documents or store the immaterial ones.

Clearing of the surplus credentials in the accurate method is vital for monetary safekeeping. So if you ever make the mistake of throwing out your expired credit cards or documents, such as bank deposit slips or other official papers that convey serious private or monetary material, then you might ruin everything and get hacked or your identity might be stolen. I won't advise you to throw out your things; I give it to you to organize your things.

**Storing your things physically**

**Cabinet**: Save different cabinets, if possible a metal one or a segment of the cabinet for piling all the aforementioned files tidily and in an easily accessible way.

**Safe**: You might purchase another small safe for storing extra vital official papers like personal or the ones that have to do with taxes. Try to get the ones that are fire resistant or water resistant.

**File management companies**: These companies offer services for keeping physical and online files for a small fee. The physical documents are stored in warehouses in various layers for protection and indexed for easy access. They also offer pick-up and delivery services and the documents will be brought within two to three days.

**Storing online**

**Computer**: This is one of the stress-free document storage solutions where your credentials willed be scanned into your laptop. The disadvantage is that one might be unable to get your documents back if the computer has problems. In order to avoid having a problem with your computer crashing, keep the documents in a hard drive. Or you can just scan the document into your email. The only problem is to avoid losing your password.

**Try the cloud storage option**: The options that allow free storage on these online options are numerous. Google Drive and Dropbox provide a free storage option, but it is limited unless you pay for a better version. Just make sure you open an account and then log into it.

## Organizing small extra Items

So, we've solved the issues with your documents and stationery at home. You can store them in way that you won't have to keep looking everywhere for grocery receipt or tax documents. It will be easy to drop all your miscellaneous things in a cupboard. The one issue is that, when you want to use something, you find it hard to get it. So how do you then deal with these problems? In this section of the book, we will move ahead and talk about miscellaneous items collectively. I will dish out some very helpful tips that will help you gather your stuff and take your house to the next level.

## Where do you keep your miscellaneous Items?

The description of miscellaneous means many items gotten from diverse sources. This English word denotes all things from books to makeup and so on. Miscellaneous stuff are small objects; however, they are important domestic items that have a tendency to overthrow your home if you are not organized. Just one object cannot cause your heart to race, but when it's plenty, these objects will cause a great problem.

## Here are examples of miscellaneous stuff:

Chargers

Manuals

Batteries

Lamp

Tickets

Shoe polish

Nail polish

Shoe brushes

Buttons

Key holders

Needle and thread

Scissors

Surge protectors

Headphones and earpieces

Extra pair of headphones

Hand Sanitizer and lotion

Envelopes

Bobby Pins

Lip gloss

Nail kit

Safety pins

Important pamphlets

Toilet rolls etc.

I know you've come to agree these items don't even follow in any form or order; that is because it is what they call miscellaneous objects. On an accurate review, though, we can arrange these objects and keep them so they can be useful when it's time to use them.

**These storage ideas can be done in two ways:**

1.  Keep this stuff in one place.

2.  Make a home toolkit.

Now, I'll go through each method and you can choose which one you think will work best for you:

**1.  Keep this stuff in one place**

- Arrange miscellaneous objects in definite collections.

For you to achieve this, you must arrange these objects in a more reasonable way. The impression here is so that you can discover a neutral theme for similar objects. You can select any kind of theme you want, as long as it looks good and reasonable to you.

Let me explain to you using this example. I'll be using electronics as an example:

**Electronic objects**

Chargers

Surge protector

Head phones

Ear pieces

Extension cords

**Document and paper objects**

Manuals, e.g., television, radio and phone manuals

Registration cards

Tickets

Receipts

**Typical household items**

Scissors

Super glue

Stamps

Envelopes

**Practical Items**

Batteries

Torchlight

Key holders

**Clothing and Shoe Repair Items**

Safety pins

Buttons

Needle

Thread
Shoe polish

**Beauty and Personal Items**

Bobby pins

Hand Sanitizer

Cuticle pusher

Lip gloss

Once you have those sorted into groups. You can now find good locations in your house and store them.

2. **Get storage options**.

After separating these items into different sections that all fit, it's time to take these home objects to the suitable part of home and try to make use of your current storage solution, for example vanity tables that contain drawers, mason jars, and containers etc. The other option is for you to make storage options. You should label the drawer or any type of storage solution you choose and get these items stored.

- **Create a household toolkit**

To use this method, you can ignore the above and try this one. But for now, no options is better than the other. With this method, you have to store these miscellaneous objects together. But with this method, you need to keep it differently and label every container and store it.

- **Arrange these miscellaneous objects into distinct collections.**

Remember, to get this done, you have to arrange these miscellaneous objects into precise sets or groups. The truth is that you can never do it the wrong or right way, unless you organize it anyhow or in a rough way. Make the collections that are most sensible to you. You will eventually discover it is useful to keep them according to the collections I made above.

- **Select a long-lasting storage place.**

Afterward, choose a room in your house for you to keep all those objects mentioned above. It's a great clue to put all these objects in one unit, such as file cupboard, safe, containers etc. There must be sufficient cabinet and units to use. After you've chosen your storage location, it is advisable to tidily organize items into bits of units or storage containers. Cautiously and tidily bind ropes, cables, and cord, and try using drawer separators and containers to hold other objects.

You might make use of big, transparent zippered nylon bags in order for you to collect objects. Last, label these items, so it's stress-free to know where objects fit.

So how do you want to arrange your miscellaneous items?

# CHAPTER TEN

# CREATING STORAGE SPACE

What do you think having or creating a storage space is all about? You see, organizing your home into neat units and making use of the space effectively isn't the only thing about home organization. Have you ever thought of creating even more space for storage? You see, unlike chapter eight, where I discussed extensively how to use enough space when your home is too big, this chapter basically teaches you how to create more space in the house, especially if you live in a cramped environment.

In this chapter, you will learn how to create minor and hard-to-reach parts of the house that you either don't presently make use of or may possibly be used more efficiently. Two key parts that could be changed into working storage space are under stairs if your home is a story-building or in the roof area (attic). There are facilities made available by experts that can make available space where nothing has been before. Under the staircase area is great for keeping jackets, Christmas adornments, vacuum cleaners and additional objects that you do not use every single day and yet you still do not have an existing storage space.

It all depends on what shape and size your roof is though. You can create a small room from the attic, you can create an office, you can create a reading room, and you can set up a shelf such that the vacant area will be transformed into a space for storing items that are used only once in a while. Accessibility can be created by installing an attic ladder, which will fold away when not in use. Otherwise, hooks and racks can be hung on the backs of most internal doors, on the side of cupboards or on shower rails. In each case, you can convert unused, empty space into storage space.

Reorganize the height of shelves in cupboards, based on the size of items you wish to store, so that available space is used more efficiently. But seriously though, if you have never used your attic or staircase space or you are moving to a new house and you need to keep it clean and organized, then stick to this section. Read it carefully and absorb every point. The first part I will talk about is the attic.

1. **Attics**: Roof spaces are commonly the utmost interesting rooms in an apartment. There are a lot of people who see them as secret rooms and a very cool place to create something; the truth is that it can actually serve as a place where you can create art, shoot pictures, and even write your books. How you use the attic depends on the flair you have. Anyway, the attic can have this awesome vibe if used well. You see, decorating and organizing the attic can be a serious nerve wrecking thing. So, you need to start trying different things so you know what works. Below, I will give you practical ideas on how to make the best of your attic and create more space in your

house. Have this at the back of your mind; the attic can be used store anything.

- **Create an office**: You can create an office out of an attic whether you work from home or not. If you don't work from home, you can redesign the place and turn it into a study room where you keep your books and writing materials. If you turn this part of the house into a study room, then you can store your books and stationery. The point of turning this part to a study room or office is to keep bookish things and still have a nice quiet time in your home. But make sure you protect your attic from too much heat and moisture.

- **Turn the attic into a bunk room**: If you live in an apartment where it has too many things, you can turn your attic into a bunk. The idea of fitting a double-decker bed can into the roof space. Moreover a bunk room and books can make a great view. You get to view your whole street and still have your bed and books stored in a roof space.

- **Create a bed that has drawers beneath it:** An additional idea you can put in your attic is to turn it into a bedroom then fix drawers beneath the bed. Seriously, having your room in an attic can be useful. Moreover you may construct shelves in the attic; hence, this will house some shelf items and create more space down in your house.

- **Construct shoe racks and bookshelf:** The roof space can be used for keeping shoes and books too. I love this mixture of both things. Moreover, you can enhance the attic with a sofa where you can take a break and read books.

- **Construct a closet and storage on option:** If you have just too many clothes and your room isn't containing it anymore, I believe it is time to turn your attic into a closet. A closet using wooden or metal rods is a great idea to fix in a roof space. The closet maybe recycled to stock clothes, especially the ones you don't plan to wear anymore. For example, your wintertime jackets can be kept in your attic. To add a twist, mix it with a closet with drawers, super fantastic idea. When you mix drawers and your closet, you will get extra space to save more clothes in the drawer. I wouldn't really advise you to keep your toiletries there, especially if you do not plan to turn it into your room.

Furthermore, you can add a mirror to spice up your room. The bottom line is that your attic will contain things you don't have to keep on the floor space of your house. Isn't that great?

- **Make an additional storage solution on the unused outside wall:** The roof space can be changed into a storage solution by making shelves that can serve different purposes. A storage container or boxes can be put on the shelf, and it can be used to save home decorations before Christmas or Halloween.

So now that's settled, I want you to go to your attic and see what you can turn it into. Remember, there's no pressure here. Even if you think it has no usefulness, you can just store things you no longer need or things you don't use every day in your roof space. The rest of the storage solutions for creating space in your house is below the staircase. The thing is, I don't even know which is more awesome, the roof space storage or under the stairs. But we can both learn ways to make your house very well-organized by using the deserted area beneath your stairways, and by what method you can create that area to work very well. Discover the numerous methods that can be taken advantage of when it comes to storage areas.

Let's see how useful under your stairways can be when it comes to storing your items.

You will seriously relish seeing various astonishing ways to make your house work just fine. One of my preferred things is converting the vacant space below your stairways into a touch of wonderful things. You ever observed your vacant space beneath your stairs? There are lots of possible vacant storage areas that are left looking useless. This is can happen in very big or small homes. Though, before some things can get on track in your vacant space beneath the stairways, whether through an expert or by you, there are things that have to happen that make your stairways harmless and architecturally thorough.

Everything is dependent on the plan of your house, and the space beneath your stairways can provide many storage solutions. Sincerely, there are very awesome ways to use the space beneath your stairs, and even if you are using it already, you can revamp your already cramped up staircase and turn it around.

**1. Turn under the stairways to a bathroom or changing room:** Just like I said earlier, creating a bathroom or powder room will work pretty well. So if you do that, then it simply means you can store some bathroom items in there. It'll be super-fun that you'd even get a bathroom downstairs, and it'll be easily accessible. This bathroom can work well when you have kids around or grandparents as guests in your house. It's just plain easy access for elderly people. Plus I've heard from several sources that, when bathrooms are on the ground floors (so far you are not breaking any building laws), it will help boost the rate at which your property will be valued by five percent. Having a bathroom underneath the stairs will provide a sense of ease even when there's one bathroom in the house already. If you plan to fix the toilet yourself, then you can search for tutorials on YouTube.

**2. Fixing up a store room under the stairs:** Building a storeroom will not only allow cherished vacant space in the kitchen, but then again it provides you with a big part for usage more than the usual kitchen cupboard. A storeroom is where you can keep absolutely anything. And I remember mentioning that canned foods can be stored in stores, so an under the stairs store room will work exceptionally well for storing canned foods. Changing your under the stairs space will provide enough liberty with the ways you work in your own kitchen. A cupboard is undoubtedly the utmost but also versatile solution, and if you get a cabinet properly, it will provide you additional storage area, but a thing that says sophisticated, practical, and properly prearranged. If you want to see strategies on ways to construct a cabinet yourself, then search YouTube videos on that.

3. **Fixing up a laundry room under the stairs:** So many new houses came with a utility area in the house. The utility room is always around the kitchen. In fact, it is connected to the kitchen and there is where your washing machines and equipment like the laundry machine and an ironing board, clothing peg and laundry detergent, etc. Actually, the laundry rooms also usually have a boiler etc. Nevertheless, if your home is small or you have no space for your machines, then changing the vacant space beneath the stairways can actually make a change. Improve the shelf to keep your detergents, and material softeners, pegs for clothes, etc. and every other laundry equipment and then use curtains to keep or hide it all.

4. **Construct drawers under the stairs:** Constructing drawers under the stairs is pretty comparable to the example in the previous option; nevertheless, certain modifications can be detected. A cabinet can accommodate shelves and drawers inside it, commonly hidden with a door. Nonetheless, an open shelf has developed over the years and is now popular, particularly in situations where you desire to show something. And creating several drawers can be valuable, depending on the things you plan to keep in them.

5. **Build a room for your pet under the stairs:** Have any pets? Maybe your cat wants to always curl next to you, especially when you

want to sleep. Perhaps it's a dog? Does your dog know anything about space and not the one that wants to sit around you, always? Why don't provide your dog its own miniature room? These small rooms provide your cherished pet space. That's like a home built in another home but specifically for dogs.

6.     **Try working from home:** Do you bring work home? Probably you've been working all day and still you needed to bring the work home, so turning under the stairways of your home into an office is a great idea. Keep this in mind though; the shape and size of your stairs will determine how this will work out for you. Dedicating a part of your home to a well-organized and structured office is one way to go. Did you know that you can actually even store your files in there too? If you have office files you want to keep, then try that space under your stairs .

7.     **Love reading? Then turn that space into a library:** Having something as personal as a library is fun. Pretty interesting if you ask me. How wonderful do you think it will be if you can create space in your house and pack those books under the stairs. Ah! Wonderful, right? Just don't pack though; neatly arrange it in that space. You can have a carpenter put up something that looks like a shoe rack or shelf and arrange your books according to color or genre. Just remember, while you make this arrangement, keep in mind that when you want to find the book you need again, you mustn't just stack books in the shelf. Arrange it wisely.

8. **Creating a reading nook under the staircase is similar in some ways. Here's how:** Just like a library, having a reading nook creates a personal and private space for yourself. You can always go to that space to relax, drink coffee, and read. You feel stressed, then just go into the reading nook to unwind. You can always find people to fix the under stair sitting area, but all in all, make sure it also serve the purpose of storing your books, especially if you do not have a bookshelf in your home. Try fitting a cabinet, shelf, drawers, and a bench where you can sit. As much as aesthetics is great, always keep in mind that storing your things is very important. It's left to you to follow all my storage advice and think of the things that actually can be stored under your stairs. Storage comes first then aesthetics later, but then again, these two things go hand in hand. Although, if you want to make your storage solution look simple, then everything will depend on you and you alone. Yes, I have gone crazy with storing my things at home, and it is entirely up to you to go crazy with pillows, blankets, fairy-lights and even paint it with a great colour. You are lucky to have that part in your home, so if you do have it, use it right, and if you do not have that space, follow the storage options I gave you up there.

9. **Want a bar in your home? Have a couple of beers and you don't want to use the space in your home for it?** How about try using under your staircase for a bar. Sometimes, having friends over can be fun. What if you have friends over who love too much fun?

What if you love too much fun too? Lol. Keeping beers in that space is a very good idea for those who want to use the space in their homes well. Having a bar at home is the coolest thing ever; you don't even have to step out in the night to go have fun in the bar anymore. Just go down the stairs of your room, get some beer, and drink. What's even more fun about this idea is that you get to use this as a storage option. Even if you have a freezer, I doubt you want to put it in your freezer. You can put a drink or two but crates of beer isn't going to look nice in your fridge. Having some sort of wet and dry bar is similar, but there's only one thing to note: wet bars have sinks with plumbing and all. You get to rinse your glasses without going to the kitchen to get it clean. Imagine you have to keep rinsing your cups after having a drink each time and then to rinse it, you have to go to the kitchen. Why not have that sink and water just under your stairs where you have your bar. It is a practical knowledge that, if your bar is in the basement for example, getting it cleaned in the kitchen after having a drink in your bar will be frustrating for you. And if you are even the type that gets easily tired, your bar will turn out to be a whole lot of mess. So therefore, if you created a bar very close to the kitchen, you might not necessarily have a sink. A dry bar is good to go. You know why it would be unreasonable to have a sink in your bar when the kitchen is nearby? You'd have to cough out extra cash for that one extra space when there is a plumbing issue. Although, if you change your space under the stairs into a bar, you must realize this will work better depending on the location of your stairs. Think about it, is it wise to create a bar down there? If you think it's actually great, then you must consider the advantages and disadvantages that come with it. Consider the distance of your planned bar to the kitchen itself. Do you really need a sink? You know your home and you know where the stairs are; you know how important that space down your stairs is. Is the wet bar that important or is the dry bar a superb ideas for your home? To furnish or not to furnish? I think furnishing will make the space compact and neat. Have a carpenter construct shelves for you, get a fridge in there, and keep in mind that the goal of this point is to teach you how to store your beer if you love drinking.

10. **You love wine? Then a rack under the space of your stairs is great**: The thing is that I don't like the idea of a bar in the house itself. If you make it work then fine. Yes, I have seen people arrange these things neatly, but it still doesn't seat well. So, if you've got a staircase, I'm sure there will be a space underneath. Why then would you keep wine in an open space and make your house look tacky when the space under your stairs can work out fine? So, I'm guessing you are having a rethink and you wish to have a lot of space in your house. Will you start one under your stairs? Yes, please do. There are so many already made wine racks created to fit into the space of a staircase, it's usually not expensive, and you will get it with a few bucks. You can as well make one from shelves you used to have at home. That is why I specifically mentioned the removal method in the first chapter. There are so many ideas of turning this space into a wine

cellar, truth be told. These ideas are countless and you can choose from any of these options. When it comes to organizing your home and going DIY, only your imagination can be limited. Just think wide, go to that space, and visualize what you would want that space to serve.

While it is a beautiful idea to bring the roof space of your home alive, there are also things you should never store up in the attic if you don't want to ruin them. Note that some of these things also depend on the way you keep them in a storage option.

1. **Photos, Documents, Artwork**

Old photos, documents, and paintings are all off limits for the attic, garage, or basement.

When keeping things in your attic, you should consider the heat coming from up there. Remember it is closer to the effect of the sun, and when you put important things there, it's possible it ends up getting ruined. Humidity, insects, rodents are among the numerous things that can ruin the important things you keep there. Photographs, artwork, documents (when stored inappropriately) are off limits. If you put your photographs in the attic, your pictures will lose its colour from humidity, light and heat, and the same goes for the rest of the items listed above.

2. **Avoid fabrics up there**

Unless you do not need your clothes again, then keeping it in the attic is a no-no. Water from a leaking roof will ruin it coupled with heat. Stuffed animals, rugs etc. can also be affected if stored in the roof space. They can lose colour from humidity and heat and get ruined by insects.

3. **Electronics**

Would you leave your phone in a place with high humidity and heat? I'm guessing that's a big no. Never leave your electronics in the attic whether old ones or new ones. Water and heat are enemies of electronics. You should find somewhere else in the house to store electronics you do not need again, and if you find them really useless, then throw them away. Also, putting flammable objects up in the roof space is very dangerous. We don't usually put into consideration the likely results of the things we keep out of sight and mind, so one could mistakenly keep flammable objects close to heat source in a roof space.

You should never store chemicals or any type of cleaning products close to a heat source. Even though you're keeping additional paint far from a gas-related object, temperature can change and change the colour of your paint. Keeping your gas cylinder up there is also pretty dangerous, especially one filled with gas. You will be risking so many things, such as lives and properties. Generally though, keep flammable objects from the attic.

## 4. **Do not keep your own food or a pet's food in the attic**

You should never store your food or a pet's where insects, rodents and humidity are common. It is not in any way healthy. Not only are you leaving your food exposed to poison, the level of moisture and heat in the attic is usually too much and might end up ruining your food. All this applies to the basement too. Although, if you have a garage that is aerated and you believe there won't be a problem, then go ahead and keep your things there. Attics and basements are off the list.

# Conclusion

Organizing your home takes more than making the surface look clean. When you have an organized environment, you will be able to enjoy your time and belongings. One of my goals for this book is to make you learn the easy ways of doing it right. Learning to make your environment have a nice, simple flow of movement and accessibility to items in your home.

Organizing your home is not difficult, but it takes practice. Practice drives you to do more for your house and to make your house more beautiful. During my learning phase of organizing the home, you must also learn to work with time. It is also very important, especially for people who are very disorganized. Time is more elusive than space, so you must know time is not what you can see. It can't be piled up like the clothes in your wardrobe or closet.

During the course of this book, you have learned so many things. Obviously, there have been parts of your house where you keep excess items. Imagine having books or any other item in your house that aren't that important lying on different spots of your home. Imagine you do not ever create the time to make your house sparkling clean. Would you like that?

You can always keep learning new things when you research and that is one of the purposes of this book. The point of learning these things is so you can look at your home differently and see what can be done about the disorganized environment. I believe, after reading the chapters carefully, you get to spot things that may have been overlooked and then consider ways to keep them neat and organized in your house. The thing I have put in mind when cleaning up my home is to find the things that can be turned into storage. I have realized over the years that even a glass cup can help to keep absolutely anything: pencils, art brushes, pens etc.

But you must realize that organization can be done only if you do research, ask professionals what they think. It doesn't stop there with this book. It helps you further to keep digging deeper and deeper so you can plan and take a line of action. It took a great deal of time for me to learn how to do these things, but it is lovely, isn't it.

What you are supposed to do is all written in the previous chapters. I have learned one thing: people are not naturally born as organized individuals. I know there are people who are always very uncomfortable when it comes to a disorganized place, but let's face the fact, no one is born an organized human. It is what we as people cultivate into habits. These habits will reflect in everything you do as a person. When you are organized, it will show how you get your work done. If you are still a student, you will know exactly when to organize your school work and get things done.

Even if you have assumed you are a disorganized person, I promise you that you will learn things differently. You will learn to plan things ahead, take notes, and forgo things that have no value for you. Anyone, I repeat anyone, can actually learn the act of organization, but this can happen only if you read the tips above and absorb them.

Organized people are always with notes, writing and observing things. Picture an office secretary or personal assistant who absolutely does not know the art of keeping things in order. Do you know how many times such a person will fail at things? Your boss has a flight in a week, you've not booked the plane, even if you booked it, you have failed to keep the ticket in an accessible place. How will your boss feel? Probably she or he will fire you. See, a person who is disorganized at home will never be organized at work. It will always show, even when they try to hide.

One of my main reasons for writing this book is to let people know how deadlines are as important as doing things right. Let's face it, only people that do well with deadlines can actually ever be organized. Someone who has a meeting but has failed to put it down will have a problem. Unless the meeting is important, then you might end up forgetting everything about it. Imagine remembering the last minute that you have that meeting and you've even had your clothes ready.

Learning organization has taught me the rules of doing things at the right time. I will never come home and drop my documents on the table then procrastinate and tell myself I can always do it later. No, organization has taught me differently. When you do things, you must do it in time and do it well. Let's make an experiment. Visualize a thing in your life that you think needs to be monitored and organized. Write down these things, put down the solutions for it, and then set a period of time you think you can get it done. If it is something you can do within an hour, then you should stand up now and do it.

Organizing is super fun, and it is what you will learn during the course of this book. Believe me when I tell you how easy it is to get lost in a pile of mess. You can learn to keep your house organized because it will reflect in your life. People who are organized keep things properly and label them. Now isn't that fun? Isn't it fun to go to a section of your house to find an item and easily find it?

One thing is to organize and store your things. In the process of organizing these things, do you ever wonder why you still scatter your household items even after organizing them? I can tell you why. You aren't making your things easily accessible. You have to put that in mind, but I promise, you will learn that in this book. You will understand the reasons storing things and finding it easily when you need them is helpful. Disorganized environments aren't good for healthy living and the same can be said for inaccessible items in the house.

# DECLUTTERING YOUR HOME

*THE SIMPLE AND COMPLETE GUIDE TO GET RID OF STUFF YOU NO LONGER USE AND REACH THE MINIMALIST LIFE YOU ARE LOOKING FOR*

**By**

**Anne Marie Rooms**

# All rights reserved. © 2019 by Anne Marie Rooms.

No part of this book may be scanned, uploaded, reproduced, distributed, or transmitted in any form or by any means whatsoever without written permission from the author, except in the case of brief quotations embodied in critical articles and reviews. Purchase only authorized electronic editions and do not participate in or encourage electronic piracy of copyrighted materials. Thank you for supporting the author's rights.

**Disclaimer**

All the material contained in this book is provided for educational and informational purposes only. No responsibility can be taken for any results or outcomes resulting from the use of this material.

While every attempt has been made to provide information that is both accurate and effective, the author does not assume any responsibility for the accuracy or use/misuse of this information. Some names have been changed and/or omitted in order to protect the privacy of certain characters in this book.

# CONTENTS

Introduction .................................................................... 134

Chapter One: Dealing With Clutter: Phase 1 .................................. 140

Chapter Two: Why Do We Keep Clutter? (Part Two) ................. 160

Chapter Three: Dealing With Clutter ........................................... 173

Chapter Four: The Journey To Minimalism: Decluttering 101 ..... 183

Chapter Five : Five Minutes!!! ..................................................... 206

Chapter Six: Deluttering As A Fashion-Loving Minimalist......... 217

Chapter Seven: Deluttering And Relationships 1: Decluttering With Your Family And Friends In The Minimalist Approach ............... 231

Chapter Eight: Deluttering And Relationships 2: Decluttering As A Minimalist Parent....................................................................... 250

Chapter Nine: Decluttering And Finances: Minimalism As A Financial Detox .......................................................................... 263

Chapter Ten: After Decluttering, What's Next? ........................... 282

Conclusion .................................................................................. 284

# INTRODUCTION

"How does this whole thing about decluttering work?"

"Taking my time to be fully into the minimalism life seems like a little too much just because I need to declutter my home."

"Decluttering seems unnecessary, because I feel like I do not need it. I could just admire the ideas of it from a distance."

"I have problems deciding what is important in my room to keep and what I should throw away."

"I am a lady of elegance and I love to live grand- with a variety of clothes, jewelry and more. As long as I can afford them, I do not need to settle for decluttering."

"I love decluttering, but I feel like trying to balance it with my responsibilities in my family would be difficult."

"I love shopping, but I really want to try this minimalist lifestyle. What do I do?"

Most times, when we think about the idea of decluttering our home, it may seem appealing. Many of us become so eager to try it because decluttering to be a minimalist is the new trend. Some of us do not, perhaps because we feel we do not need it. The rest of us are indifferent about it, because we are probably not sure if we want it or because the hype around it appears to be over the top. Either way, all the opinions I listed above fall under these three choices. For me, it was basically all three.

Do not get me wrong. I liked the idea of decluttering to live the minimalist lifestyle. But, I liked extravagance more. I wanted to live the minimalist lifestyle so badly, yet I did not want to go through with it. I could not imagine the fact that I would have to control what I shop for at the mall. Who would want that? Definitely not I...back then.

You see, that's where our major problem lies. As we make an attempt to declutter, some difficult items might slow us down. They are not basic things we need, but for some reason or the other, we are not quite ready to part with them. Because of that, we start to lose the motivation, and we conclude that we can't be minimalists after all. But don't worry. I've got your back. Throughout the chapters of this book, we will be going through how to glide right over that trouble spot and keep going smoothly.

When I finally decided to become a minimalist, I got confused about where to start or how to start. I read several posts and followed people who were totally into it. I wrote down important ideas I could add to suit my interest, applied them, and even turned it into a fun game at some point. I would tell my friends that, if I was not applying the things I put in place for myself or if they caught me violating them, I would give my pretty clothes away or give them money. Other times, I would strike a bet with my sister that, if I did not follow it, she would take any clothing she wanted. It seemed pretty silly, but it really helped me in the long run.

It was like a challenge I had to win. I knew there was no way I was going to give my clothes or shoes or jewelry to anyone unless I was forced to do so. I knew that I also would not want to lose money to a bet, so I was cautious. I would check up on how much progress and mistakes I had made, what I needed to improve on, and the lessons I learned. There were times that I gave away some things I wasn't keeping to friends and charity shops or sent some things for recycling. There were also times that I gave them away because I lost the bet. It was not always so easy, but it was worth it.

With time, I became better and the best part...I saved more money! I had more money to myself. I was able to buy other things that were more important. Instead of spending my hard-eared money on frivolous purchases, I was even able to invest in better things. I also started to see the world differently, and my principles about some things changed. The whole process of removing all material possessions I no longer required from my life taught me a number of lessons.

I know what you are thinking: "Doesn't all of this seem too serious?" Decluttering your home to have a minimalist lifestyle is as simple as breathing. This book is not going to dictate what you must do. This book is filled with creative ideas that I gained from my personal experience. All I want is to share my ideas and knowledge with people. I just want to inspire others to be happy. I want to inspire people to pursue minimalism, to live more by owning less. So, I am writing a book.

This book will assist you with learning and practicing at your pace, until it becomes part of you. It will help you solve time management problems. Decluttering your home to become a minimalist is not particularly for any specific person. It is for everyone- men and women of all ages and lifestyles. If you are considering trying this after carrying out your thorough research, this book is for you.

If you just heard about it, or perhaps you have been quietly watching others live with less for some time now and you are ready to jump in, this book is for you.

If you are trying to stay consistent on your mission to declutter and minimize, this book is for you too.

If you have a problem letting go of your belongings and it is becoming a hurdle for you to complete your decluttering process, this book is for you.

If you are thinking of how to start as a parent or how to sustain your minimalist lifestyle, this book is for you and for every other person who loves the concept of Decluttering and Minimalism.

There are no compulsorily fixed procedures or guidelines you need to follow. But if you want to go into it, you need to be well-rounded about it. You need all the guidance you can get if you are shaping your life to be more with less.

That being said, it is almost never an overnight transformation. It takes as long as it takes for each person. So, do not be discouraged or worried if things are not going as planned at first. The only three things that should matter to you are: Time, Consistency, and Commitment.

There is never a perfect time or way to start. Take one step at a time, like the phrase "baby steps". And if you can, start it all at once. The moment you start to work on these ideas, you will begin to alter the course of your home, and perhaps even your life, in a positive way.

I hope these ideas help you as much as possible, and I hope you put them into practice and share your knowledge with other people.

# CHAPTER ONE: DEALING WITH CLUTTER: Phase 1

**WHY DO WE KEEP CLUTTER? (Part One)**

Your rooms are filled and keep growing with stuff that you feel you might need just in case- because they are all things that you treasure or store in collections. But then, you wonder what is causing the clutter in your house.

The sight of your garage or the kitchen feels too suffocating or overwhelming for you, but you are too busy to deal with it. It's like the day you finally decide that you finally want to deal with the clutter, you get called into work or by someone else for an emergency or something urgent.

You love your home, and you put in so much effort and time to ensure it is taken care of. Yet, you cannot seem to fathom what is making your garage and other parts of your apartment look like dumping grounds.

Have you ever come back home after having a busy day that had you on your toes and you are so stressed? Then, your eyes go to your paper trails (mail and magazines) that are stacked up and overflowing around the house. And, you are like..."That cannot be organized...not today." Again, the procrastination does not stop, because your mind does not want to picture that image of you dealing with the day, the next day or another day.

Do not worry. We are never really at fault most of the time. In our minds, we have the best intentions of actually decluttering our homes to live a life of minimalism. However, reality could differ from our ideas and stand against our intention. Then, we realise we cannot help ourselves. Sometimes, it is alright if it happens and our stuff is messed up everywhere or too much at times. Read that again. Read that again and hold on to that word **"sometimes"**.

It is okay if we give in to the clutter in our homes occasionally; however, it is not good if we make it our lifestyle. Although we may not be conscious of it, clutter affects most parts of our lives. Our clutter tells a lot about us. It may look like quite a handful of items flying around, yet it could have depths of meaning. So I ask: What does your clutter represent? What does it say about you? How does it affect you? Are they simply your possessions or are they actually possessions that you are attached to or more?

The truth is we need to ask ourselves these questions if we want to work on removing clutter in our home. Applying techniques, approaches, methods and any other procedure to make our homes clutter-free will only remain ineffective, unless we tackle the problems causing us to have or keep clutter. If we ignore or stay ignorant about the reasons our home is not transforming the way we want it to be (uncluttered), we will be reverting to square one. Do you know what square one is? The problem. This leaves us with the question, why do we have/keep clutter?

There have been different theories that center on clutter. For instance, Teri Lynn Mabbitt, a professional organizer in Denver, believes there are four categories of clutter.

**Technical:** Clutter that causes space restrictions and an overall lack of storage space.

**Life changes:** Clutter caused by a new baby, a death in the family, a move or anything that has thrown a life out of balance.

**Behavioral/psychological:** Clutter caused by depression, attention deficit disorder, low self-esteem or lack of personal boundaries.

**Time/life management:** Clutter caused by the need for better planning.

Out of these four, she says the behavioral/psychological-driven clutter is the hardest to solve. These theories are right and fully fit in to different practical situations. But as much as they are right, they imitate the three familiar patterns of clutter: Physical clutter, Emotional clutter and Mental/Psychological clutter. No matter the theory, they all fall back on these three patterns, which is why I would like to categorise the several reasons we keep or have clutter into these patterns and discuss how to overcome them.

## PHYSICAL CLUTTER

### 1. The word "Clutter" is not properly understood

The word "clutter" is pretty common, so we expect that people understand it when we say the word. Other times, we use the word even for the wrong things. Our misuse leads us to misunderstanding what should be referred to as clutter and what should not be referred to as clutter.

That being said, the question we should ask ourselves is: What is Clutter?

Clutter is the excessive amount of anything that does not belong in a space. It does not have to be that pile of mess on the counter. It could be unfinished house projects or repairs that do not belong there. Anything that exists as the effect of the decisions that we postpone is clutter. When you understand what clutter is in relation to decluttering, you will be able to identify what your clutter is in your home.

So, our clutter differs from others. What we regard as clutter may not be clutter to other people. Clutter does not only include stuff that has been overused or things we outgrew. Some clutter should be thrown out. Some should be properly taken care of so they would cease to be clutter. Some should be moved to a better place at home. Some should probably be given away because they have never really been used.

This is why it is important for you to understand what qualifies as clutter in your home. Your clutter may be different from your friend's clutter. Understand what your clutter is. If you understand what your clutter is, it will be easier to identify it.

On the other hand, it is possible that you may have a hard time identifying it regardless of how long you try to understand it. This might be because you lived with clutter for so long that it grew on you. You gradually lose sight of it, and you no longer see it as clutter. Not to worry, there are other ways to sense the clutter in your home. Aside from understanding what it is, you could invite people over- I mean your friends, your boss, colleagues or a friend with a toddler. Invite people who are not too familiar with your home, considering the fact that those who frequently visit may be blind to the clutter. Observe their perception about your house. Their comments would express a lot about how other people see your home. From there, you can tell what could be changed or gotten rid of.

Also, you could take pictures or videos of your rooms. Looking at your room through pictures or videos could make it very noticeable. It will give you a fresh take on the uncluttering process.

## 2. You have too much stuff that you do not need

At early stages of our lives, we are taught that having 'more' is better than having less. As a result, you keep things you do not need. You keep things because you think you will need them again in the future. You keep things because you think they have value or just because you like them. This is how we give in to **aspirational clutter**; clutter that exists as the things you aspire to use but end up shrinking storage spaces in your home.

You know that you have too much stuff, but you choose not to get rid of it. Instead, it takes over your life until you cannot remember the last time you saw the floor of your pantry, office or the top of your dresser. And, finding your things gets harder by the day.

Maybe 'more' is good, but there is a limit to having more too. When 'more' becomes too much, it is out of your control. Loss of control over our possessions is what births clutter. Clutter makes things difficult to do. Having too much seems like an obvious and straightforward reason for the clutter, but it is one of those reasons that we commonly have too much trouble with.

You see, clutter comes with a cost. It impedes your time, your space at work or at home- basically your life. Why? Because you keep accumulating too much stuff and not enough is going out. There is too much clutter here and there. Storing them in boxes is not going to change the fact that the clutter needs to be gotten rid of. Keeping your possessions in check is advisable for you and your home. So, if you want to be a minimalist, it is necessary to take out as much clutter as you let in your home.

**3. You do not put things away**

Another obvious reason you may be drowning in your possessions is that you do not discard them. Before you drop that item somewhere else, ask yourself where it truly belongs. Everything should have a home. It could be tough putting things away if they do not have a place to go. Designate a "home" for your items. It can be as simple as a drawer that all items of a specific type go in. Or you can get storage solutions suited to specific needs. The point is to have a specific place to put your items.

## 4. You do not follow through with thorough cleaning or organizational routines

Setting up routines or clutter busters through a full-scale cleaning routine is essential for your home. When you establish such a routine, it would be easy for you to clear the clutter at your own speed.

It is always so tempting to put things at any place close to your reach. If there are no simple organizational systems set in place in your home, disorganization is inevitable- and so is clutter. Resist the temptation to put items at wrong places just because they are easy for you to access. Do not turn the wrong spaces to storage for the wrong items.

## 5. You are a Procrastinator

Procrastination can result in cluttered spaces. When we procrastinate, it strangely feels good. Do you know why? Because we feel we are handling our responsibilities and priorities well. We have this sensation that we are still at the top of our situation. The sad truth is we might not actually be where we think we are. Procrastination kills productivity. The more we delay, the more we hang ourselves out to dry.

Let's create a vivid image. Your shoe rack is overflowing, the dining room table holds a week's worth of mail and bills, the stairs are hitting a stumbling block. You spot the little mess, but it does not seem cringe worthy yet. So, you put off the task to organize it until the weekend or 'some other time'. The pile of mess keeps getting larger and larger. The 5 to 7-minute task gradually turns into a project of 4 hours or more. But, all of this could have been avoided if you had just dealt with the little mess from the start.

When we procrastinate, we tend to lose more money. Think about the accuracy in this. If I go for shopping without planning what I would be buying, I'll end up buying more than what I can afford. I might waste money on clothes or shoes that I would lose interest in after wearing them on a few occasions.

## 6. You get too much stuff you do not need

Being indecisive about what new items should serve you in the long term could be responsible for most of the clutter that enters your apartment. We buy a mountain of things that we do not need or use often. It tends to fall between one of these three sides:

*Side 1:*

Those who buy new stuff because they can't find the old ones. Their closets are overflowing with too many clothes. But, instead of dealing with the clutter, they just buy new items. Even when they avoid dealing with such clutter by storing and labelling it, it does not solve the underlying issue.

*Side 2:*

Those who buy new items based on their fickle interests. They either buy based on what ads they see on TV or something else. They buy the latest creams or printers that were recently advertised on TV or they take one pottery class and buy a whole pottery set.

A week after, it's just two or three classes on cooking, and they are buying too many cooking accessories they won't even be using throughout the year. The next month, it's dancing or painting classes. And, their houses are going to keep getting stuffed with new items that they do not need because of interests that they do not stick to.

*Side 3:*

Those who get too thirsty for freebies. It is normal if we love freebies. I mean I love freebies. Getting them obviously saves my life financially. But, if the items I got were not free, would I still buy them for a great deal anyway? If I bought that free makeup, would it be worth it? Is it ok if I get these bonuses outside my shopping list? Is it ok if I love freebies to the point where I cannot control or resist what would suit my interest in the long term? We need to ask ourselves these questions to be sure we are not encouraging aspirational clutter.

It seems satisfying to justify the free items we get on a financial basis, rather than the reality of how useful it would be on a regular basis. If it is not useful, then our homes are better off without it- because taking it in would mean crowding our storage spaces. In spite of that, it is difficult to restrain from getting free items that could turn into potential clutter, and it is much more difficult to get rid of them when they become clutter.

## 7. You might just be naturally messy

At times, there is really no reason for the clutter aside from the fact that you are a messy person. You are not bothered by the dirty dishes that have been used in the sink or the piles of clothes that you need to put up.

Being naturally messy makes your home easily cluttered. You seem to be wired that way, so you are comfortable with the mess. Keep living in your own skin, but reaching a breaking point would be better for your home.

## 8. You do not know how to maintain things

Deciding on how to maintain things or the period of time (how long) we are to maintain our possessions can be confusing for many homes. It's hard to determine what should be thrown away, sold out, given out or kept in our closets. Ginny Snook Scott says that when people do not have any methodology of when and where to let go of things, they tend to end up as clutter by default. It is crucial that we do not mix up knowing how to keep things properly with knowing when to let go of them. Maintaining our possessions includes both, but it focuses more on the latter.

## 9. Your Life is too occupied

When your life is too occupied, it means that you have an extremely busy life or your work takes so much of your time that dealing with your clutter is the last thing you want to do. If this is the reason your clutter keeps building up, it means your life is so occupied that it might be getting to the extent of chaos.

If you are too busy between catching up with work, family dinner, your friend's baby shower or your relative's birthday party, then you might be neglecting vital parts of your life- including your home. Having too much clutter might simply mean that you need to take a step back and slow down so you have time to get organized again. You might be overworking yourself, and you are just not aware of it.

**10. You are a Collector**

Oftentimes, if you love having collections of items, you could end up having a clutter problem. There's nothing wrong with collecting cool stuff and enjoying the view when you display them. All the same, it would do your home a lot of good if you downscale your hobby of collecting things to only things that you feel are very relevant and things that beautify your home. If you cannot remember some of those things you have in your collection, you might want to start reconsidering whether they should stay in the house. Do not wait till things get out of hand before you are forced to declutter.

**11. You are a perfectionist**

It sounds funny hearing that being a perfectionist could lead to clutter, because a perfectionist is supposed to be this neat and organized person who loves to tidy up at every possible time. But, what we don't know is that trying to be perfect in everything could make us feel inadequate for no reason. The downside to being a perfectionist is that, when we don't have time to do things the way we want them to be, we would rather not do them until we have that time. We feel not doing them the 'perfect' way would mess up our standards.

It does not have to be perfect all the time. Instead of waiting for the right time to organise your home, you could start with few minutes of your free time one time or another. Focus on making them better and more organized than it was before and not 'perfect'. One step at a time, so you don't turn out to be too perpetual in your decluttering. If you need help with starting small, you could follow the different five-minute tasks in the next chapter.

## 12. You are lazy

Being lazy can lead to cluttered spaces. I won't say that I'm not guilty of this one, because it used to happen to me when my house was always jam-packed with stuff. It still does happen to me but not like before. Learning to declutter in order to live the minimalist lifestyle subconsciously teaches you to be disciplined. Take time to take care of your home. When you do that, you get to watch your favorite TV show in your neat, clutter-free home. You get to laze around all you want without staring at the disturbing sight of clutter.

## 13. You Are Not Using Clutter Terminators

What are clutter terminators? Containers, trays, bins, baskets, jars, and hooks are all examples of clutter terminators, because they take up items like pieces of mail and make them look organized. They sort them into groups and remove or reduce any potential clutter.

## 14. Your Fears

The whole task of decluttering can be scary when we make ourselves believe that it is. Worrying about how to unclutter makes us fear if we can actually do it at all. Therefore, instead of doing it at all, we just choose not to. Here's one thing.

Before you overthink how to start, if you'll get through the voluminous clutter, how about you just do it without worrying? Will we ever get through this massive pile of junk? Start anywhere if you are afraid that you might not succeed in finishing it. And before you know it, you'll take care of it much better than you expected.

**15. You are used to it**

If you live in a house filled with clutter, and you don't see the need to clear your storage spaces, it might be because you lived with clutter for so long that you see it as normal.

16. Other times, you may just be going through a distinct stage in your life when things start to change, like having a baby, a new job, moving to a new home or going through financial lapses. When we go through this transition, we are likely to tell ourselves that we'll figure it out by the time things settle down.

**EMOTIONAL CLUTTER**

**1. You are sentimental**

I'm sorry to break this to you, but being sentimental can be the cause of your cluttered spaces. It means you hold on to things with sentimental value and that you have trouble letting things go. You get emotionally attached to your possessions too easily and unconsciously keep too much stuff around the house.

It is not a flaw; it is simply the way you are wired. You express your love for and appreciation of people around you through these items. I can tell that your love language would be gift-giving.

But there comes a time when these items get out of control, and it will be so overwhelming that you have to decide what to keep and what not to keep. In times like this, keep what is truly meaningful and assure yourself that those items are not enough to express how much a past event or a person means to you. Do not get around it by hiding them or separating them from the rest of the clutter. You'll only be stressing yourself and giving you more work to do later.

The beautiful memories those items bring will always be in your heart. I'm sure those people you hold dear to you would understand that too. When you start your decluttering process, and you fear that you might want to hang on to those items again, set a playlist particularly for your cleaning. It would enliven your mood and lift your spirit.

## 2. You are depressed

Depression can be another emotional cause of clutter. When your mental health is lacking, clutter is bound to appear. Your mind affects your mood, and your mod affects how you react to your physical environment. So, if you realise that you're hoarding a lot of personal issues and you find it hard to organize stuff, and then your clutter keeps suffocating your office or your home, please take care of your mental health.

## 3. You do not want to move on

Having trouble moving on from the past can contribute to clutter too. For some people, moving on means accepting change, and not everyone likes the idea of change or the feeling it gives them. Instead, they live in the past and fear that moving on would be too much for them to handle. These emotions could affect our living spaces and result in cluttered spaces that we hesitate to clear out.

Sadly, keeping clutter in your home because you are afraid of moving on won't give you that feeling of peace and happiness that an uncluttered home gives. You need to free up those tight emotions so you can breathe. Sometimes, the best thing to do is to blend with where the change takes you.

## 4. You feel guilty

There is a thin line between feeling guilty and being sentimental about your possessions. Guilt, in this context, is the fear of losing something because of what it represents to someone else, while being sentimental means being fearful of losing something because of what it might mean to you.

Guilt could be the hesitant feeling you get when you think of throwing that cookery book that holds all your family's traditional recipes, because you feel you don't need it. It may also be the fact that we contemplate throwing away some things, because that would be us wasting money. So we hold onto them to justify our guilt. It may even come as regret, when we feel we shouldn't have tossed away an item a while ago. As a result, we start punishing ourselves with guilt for what we tossed out of the house.

**5. You are too nostalgic**

No offence, but keeping all your clothes from that camping or the Christmas gift from ten years ago or something else that seemed eventful to you isn't going to take you back in a time capsule and bring back your golden experience. It's nice to be nostalgic about certain things, but don't let your love of the past keep you from living your best life in the future. Get rid of the things that are cluttering up your home and keep the items you really love.

Now that you have read all about every possible reason you physically and emotionally keep clutter, take time to study yourself and your clutter. If you can, keep notes on what clutter you have and try to link it with these reasons. After reflecting on it, what next? Do you just identify them and stay silent? Not at all, keep reading the next chapters. In Chapters two and three, you will find out that there are other overwhelming reasons we keep clutter and how we can rise from them no matter what.

**Time Management Ninja (2018). 7 Reasons Why You Are Drowning in Clutter. Retrieved from**

**https://timemanagementninja. com/2018/01/7-reasons-why-you-are-drowning-in-clutter/**

**Malissa Micheals (2017). 4 Reasons Why You Have a Clutter Problem and How to Overcome It. Retrieved from**

**https://www.google.com/amp/s/www.lifestorage.com/blog/organization/four-reasons-why-you-have-a-clutter-problem/amp/**

**Francine Jay (2019). Parents. Retrieved from**

**https://www.parents.com/parenting/better-parenting/advice/decluttering-secret-lightly-excerpt-miss-minimalist/**

# CHAPTER TWO: WHY DO WE KEEP CLUTTER? (Part Two)

The reasons we keep clutter are not restrained to physical or emotional attachments alone. Our reasons could be psychologically induced or mentally induced. A couple of scientific studies and researches have proven that the proportion of clutter in your home is highly equivalent to the stress we experience at home. Clutter contributes to the stressors we get affected with. For this reason, most people with cluttered homes are prone to more fatigue and stress.

## PSYCHOLOGICAL/MENTAL CLUTTER

### 1. You are not setting boundaries

Lack of boundaries can lead to clutter. How? A lot of times, we think the clutter is only there because we do not restrict what comes in and what should not get in. Is it those piles of stuff your friends asked you to keep for them because they could not get a perfect space for them yet? Or they probably asked you to keep them in your home for just a little while until they can sort it out. And, you keep them for just a while, then some months and then a year later, it's still in your home. But then, you just want to be there for your friends and please them so they can be happy, right?

However, do you know that, when we do not set boundaries to those piles of stuff that generate clutter, it may mean that we need to sort our personal lives before starting with the clutter? It feels nice when you help out with things from your friends or when you stretch yourself to be there for your family. It shows that you value your relationships above all. Notwithstanding, it may be more difficult to get rid of gifts from people if you are not so good at it. Throwing away gifts that we do not need or use can make us seem disloyal to the giver. Yet, do those gifts define you? Are you happy? Do you have time for yourself too? Perhaps you are bothered that people around you will be judgmental.

It all comes down to self-worth. Self-worth can be very tricky. Having self-worth means we respect the people around us and would do anything just to be there for them but not to the extent of solely depending on them to make us happy or feel loved and appreciated.

Low self-worth is what results from people wanting to please others at the expense of their happiness. I'm not saying you should not please your aunt if she gives you gifts constantly. I'm not saying that you shouldn't appreciate the souvenirs you get at work every month from your colleagues. What I am saying is, if it gets to that point where it gets excessive and starts to build mental clutter, you should be able to control it and tell your colleagues, your aunt, or your friends politely that you care about them, but what they are doing makes you uncomfortable. I hope that makes sense.

**2. Your life is out of balance**

Decluttering sometimes might not be the problem. It might be the fact that you can't seem to control a particular hobby of yours or activity that you do and then it takes up the major space in in your life and leaves the rest unattended to. It in turn manifests physically. Probably, you love going out for social events, but you focus too much on that and then find out that you are not balancing it with other parts of your life- work, family and others.

If this is you right now, you might want to rethink how much you do that activity or hobby that you love. Stay on top of it; otherwise, it would reflect in your home. Set dates when you get to do what you want to limit yourself from doing them compulsively. There needs to be that balance.

**3. You've gone through life challenges**

The challenges we struggle with can affect the process of letting go of our unwanted and unused possessions. When we are bereft /mourning the loss of someone, when we experience a traumatic situation, when we suffer an ailment or sickness, divorce or even retirement, our desire to scale things down in our home becomes drained/sapped. We may feel so suffocated by the grief or the pain that we can't help but ignore or be distracted from our surroundings at that period. As we stay frozen in time, our possessions keep growing with neglect. And so, the neglect of our possessions starts to take its toll and turns to clutter.

For the same reason, that challenge might be an emotional burden like depression or loneliness. Shutting ourselves out from the world can also be the reason for the clutter in our homes too.

If you relate with these reasons, do something about it. Meet a therapist or join a support group to get on the right track. Get help and seek healthy advice from people around you.

## 4. Your Self-worth

I know I talked about how self-worth could affect you setting boundaries to things, but the representation self-worth embodies comes in facets. Self-worth comes as three major things: our values & beliefs, our insecurities, and our pasts.

**What do we value and what do we believe in?**

As humans, we value a lot of things differently based on the beliefs we have. So, whatever we value or believe in defines our self-worth unconsciously. For example, some of us value the approval of people, because we believe that it certifies the decisions we make. This is why we may find ourselves pleasing people with what we have. When we start to have clutter in our home, we may realise that most of them are items people recommended for us, not really what we wanted.

Some of us value our appearance because we believe clothes shape us and shape the impression people have of us. As a result, when we have more clothes around the house as clutter, it seems normal, because it's where our self-worth lies.

On the other hand, some of us value success more, which may be the reason we find it difficult to declutter those high school certificates or awards we won in college, even after we retire. To us, these objects are solid proof of our achievements that, if thrown away, could reduce our self-worth by making us feel less successful.

Either way, when we resolve to purge our mental space and our self-worth of this clutter, we help ourselves. We cut off toxic things and people that we place our value in and become better versions of ourselves.

**What are our insecurities?**

Our insecurities also measure our self-worth. It's simple.

Too many insecurities+ Substantial clutter= Low Self-worth

Little or no insecurities+ Less/no clutter= High Self-worth

What leads to insecurity? Our actions. On several occasions, our insecurities are not from the clutter we have; it's from what we do with them. Do we deal with our clutter by running away from it? Or do we face it squarely? Do we hold it close and depend on it to be happy? Or do we push it away to focus on things that make us happy?

The more we keep clutter, the more we nurture fears, worries, and doubts in us. The sad part is that insecurity actually feeds on these three things. When we worry about our colleagues having nicer clothes and getting more compliments at work, we doubt ourselves, then we worry about our clothes, and then we fear what people might think about our clothes. So, we shop for so many clothes just to fill in that gap. For some time, it works, but it does not last. Then we shop for more to boost our self-worth again, and we end up going through the same circle again and again. That's how we build insecurities for ourselves, and then the clutter starts to come in.

At times, it may not even be our colleagues at work. It may be what we think of ourselves- the unhealthy ideas we put in our heads about our body or our social life. An example is when we keep so many things in our bathroom or our living room or our bedroom. We may not be conscious of the clutter, meaning anything that pertains to our personal lives. But do you know that having clutter in the bedroom could mean a person could be having intimacy or gender issues? Funny, right? But it's true. Our clutter could represent what we are insecure about. And by insecure I mean, doubting, worrying and fearing things that damage our self-worth.

Low self-worth leads to hoarding, cluttering, anti-social behaviors, obsessive shopping or negative thoughts. Low self-worth may be self-induced, but from the way I see it, it's mostly induced by society. The society we live in bamboozles us into thinking that we can only be happy and accepted when we are rich, successful, beautiful, and exceptionally perfect in all we do.

It's like the principle of the survival of the fittest. Only the ones at the top of the food chain are worthy of being recognized. The rest are considered worthless. We see it in those ads and commercials that advertise the perfect skin lotion or the perfect body or the perfect face for the perfect makeup products. We are convinced that we can only earn self-worth by gaining material things, because more possessions means more worth in society.

That destructive notion is what leads us to buy and accumulate our homes with more items to compensate for the feeling of unworthiness. It's that feeling of low self-worth that leads to our clutter problems. All of these things never really last. They may make us feel good about ourselves for some time, but that's the only satisfaction we are ever going to get. Nothing more. Accumulating clutter won't fix your problems or help you feel important and competent.

**What memories do we keep of our past?**

Clutter can be a lot of things. But one of the things that clutter majorly represents is our inability to deal with the past. When we lose someone or something, and all that's left is a fragment of that person or that thing, we tend to keep them to remind ourselves of that memory. Doing this infers that we are not ready to let go yet. So if you keep some items in the attic or in the basement, that's a hint that you might still be clinging to the past.

The memories we hold onto from the past could also mean that we are afraid of change. The fear of change is caused by our inability to let go of the past. But fearing change could be in three different forms.

First, the fear of change might not even be based on a fragment of something we lost. Now this is where self-worth comes in. When we do not relieve ourselves of the past through the clutter in our home, it is only because those things are part of what molds our self-worth. When we see those items, we are reminded of the time we felt we were loved, appreciated and worthy. So, holding onto it takes us back to that time over and over. It might be that award we got in college or in high school as an athlete or as the school president. Instead of staying in the past, why don't you celebrate the present and little successes you have each time your family stays happy or you achieve another project at your workplace?

Second, being afraid of change might denote that we fear what would happen when we remove the clutter that we are used to. In a way, it's similar to fearing change too. It's more like fear of the unknown. Would it make us feel safe, empty or different in an unpleasant way? Would it boost or reduce our self-worth?

Last, being afraid of change might portray our fear of failure. Are you afraid of taking risks? Do you prefer to play safe in and stay in your comfort zone regardless of what you do? It's not wrong to stay safe, but it might not be healthy for you if that applies to following opportunities, dreams and decisions that could be good for you. If we tend to be too indecisive or too cautious about a lot of things, those dreams and life lasting decisions we take so seriously might be the end of us. Sometimes, we just need to live in the moment and decide that we are tackling all that clutter today. Setting a three-month plan just declutter your home is really not necessary. Taking time to contemplate whether or not to declutter isn't necessary either. Act quickly and start shaping your home into the clutter-free home you need.

Fearing failure could occur differently though. Perhaps you had a relationship in the past that you felt did not really end well. You probably tell yourself that you're over it, but the last gift you got from him before you broke up says otherwise. It could even be the unfinished task you took up at the time your business was thriving. But you fear that discarding it will mean you failed to accomplish your goal, and that would hurt your pride, so you keep it. Instead of moving on, you hope to beat it, since you want things to be the way they were back then- when your business was thriving and you were happy and successful. How long will you keep hoping to do things just to save a past that is really not worth saving?

**Our happiness and self-worth should not be weighed by these things. Having things around for keepsakes does not make us feel that sense of happiness, security, love or comfort permanently. It's all a facade, which is why you should not depend on your possessions, your insecurities, your past or those toxic values and beliefs. None of these things change or affect your worth.**

**Push that button and eliminate that fear that is making you doubt yourself and procrastinate. You are not a lost cause, and you are**

***strong enough to adapt to anything. You are capable of moving on, so do not feel like you cannot cope if you do. Face your clutter squarely, work it out and watch how your low self-worth heals gradually.***

**HOW DO WE PREVENT OR CURB HOARDING?**

Hoarding is a common notion that is given less attention than it deserves. Apart from the fact that it alters how people express their emotions, hoarding could be a cause of clutter in one's home. There are few cases where the reason for the clutter might be because some of us are just hoarders. Hoarding is said to be triggered by Obsessive-Compulsive Disorder (OCD), Obsessive-Compulsive Hyperactivity Disorder (OCHD) or Obsessive Attention Deficit Disorder (OADD). These disorders result in people being genetically pre-disposed to living as pack rats. Even as scary as these disorders may seem, there are still ways this impairment can be controlled.

First, we need to be able to differentiate what hoarding is from what it isn't. Most people tend to have hoarding tendencies, but they are not hoarders. If you see symptoms, check yourself with a health expert before it is too late.

Second, declutter at a slow pace. Do not use the blank page method, by throwing out everything at once. It might have a negative effect on you later. Go through the clutter one by one each week. But as you declutter each part of your room, deal with it all at once, so you won't have to hesitate the next time or go through the stress of decluttering the same thing over and over again. For those collections with multiple things, scale them down and reduce them to just one or two pieces. Toss the unused or unnecessary items away and put them in a box to donate.

Annie-Marie Gambelin (n. d.). The psychology of clutter: Why we hold unto 'stuff'– and what that may be teaching our kids. Retrieved from

https://www.google.com/amps/s/www.mother.ly/the-psychology-of-clutter why-we-hold-unto-stuff

Susan Biali Haas (2011). What Your Clutter, Big or Small, Is Trying to Tell You. Retrieved from

https://www.google.com/amp/s/www.psychologytoday.com/us/blog/prescriptions-life/

The Denver Post (2008). The Psychology of Clutter. Retrieved from

https://www.google.com/amp/s/www.denverpost.com/2008/01/23/the-psychology of clutter/amp/

BESTLIFE (2017). 15 Things Your Clutter Says About You. Retrieved from https://bestlifeonline.com/15-things-your-clutter-says-about-you/

Berni Sewell (n. d.). 6 eye-opening reasons why we accumulate clutter (and how to finally let go). Retrieved from

https://increasingselfworth.com/6-reasons-accumulate-clutter/

# CHAPTER THREE: DEALING WITH CLUTTER

## Phase 2

**HOW DO WE SEE CLUTTER?**

Having too many things around can be a burden in your home, but it can be eye-opening knowing why they exist in the first place. Knowing your clutter comes before any other thing. It is the first stage of your decluttering process. You can't declutter or be a clutter buster without identifying what your clutter is.

However, how do you become aware of any of those things, when you can't even recognise what your clutter is in the first place? How do you clear the stuff you don't need when you do not know what to get rid of? It can be confusing to determine whether what we see or intend to put away is the real clutter.

Perhaps, it could be because we walk in and out of our houses every day, and we become so used to the clutter around us. Perhaps we are just so good at treating clutter like it does not exist, or we are just wired to be blind to clutter. The truth is our clutter varies, and as a result, distinguishing clutter from what is useful in our homes tends to be tough. What I consider as clutter may differ from what you have as clutter. So, what you should ask yourself is, "What is clutter to you?"

Even as our clutter is not the same, there is still a common ground. The clutter in our home are the things that take up storage space and leave it messy or untidy. Whatever occupies your room as unused or unnecessary, whatever makes your room look unkempt or clustered is clutter. The same thing goes for me. The stuff that contribute to the clutter might be different, but the purpose it serves in your home and every other person's home will always be the same. For example, I have an old printer that I love because I bought it at a very affordable price at the time. The printer was really useful for me when I needed it, but it's already getting too old, and it's crystal clear that I need to put it away. Yet, I just can't think of throwing it away, so I keep it. My house is stuffed with so many things, and I just can't see what it looks like. It keeps getting worse, but I can't fathom why. I know everywhere feels suffocated, and I want to do something about it. All the same, I don't understand why my house is cluttered. The only things I have around are the things I love, including my printer. How do I know what to get rid of or recognise what isn't useful anymore?

For many reasons, we get stuck in this situation and have trouble determining what clutter is in its different form. But, the main reasons we face this problem is because of our lack of control and decisiveness. When we cannot discipline ourselves to clear everything that could possibly lead to clutter, it could be because we cannot control ourselves to stay true to the cause of sustaining a new home. Being indecisive affects the way we make our choices about how organised and clutter free our homes should be- including our lives.

Not to worry, there are primary guides you can follow to help identify what is clutter and what isn't.

## A). Ask yourself the crucial questions

One of the things that could help you in dealing with your clutter is asking yourself key questions.

## Do I need this?

Just because you seldom use that item on very sparse occasions does not mean you need it. You need to observe how such item corresponds with your interests and lifestyle. Do you enjoy using them? Are they essentials that you can't do without? If they are so important and impossible to put away, then that's an item you need.

Do you have an expensive coffee maker, regardless of the fact that you hate coffee? Then, you should not keep it around. Give it out to someone who loves coffee and sees it as a must-have every day.

If you don't use it every day, you're not going to need that item later; therefore, you should know that it is clutter and it should be gotten rid of.

**Why do I need it?**

If you do not have a rational or certain reason why you need that item, you might want to move on from having a cluttered home to having a clutter-free home. Supposing I found some containers I haven't used in a long time and I can't tell if I would use them, yet I still feel that I need to keep stuff- that would be me harboring clutter.

For as long as it does not add value to your life, it is clutter. Even so, it pays to be conscious of the kind of things we place value on. Our value meter can be tricky. You might not like decorative objects, yet the thought of you decluttering them could make you suddenly value it and not want to throw it away. Just because those containers seem useful for us does not mean we should keep them, even when they are getting too much. If they don't spark joy, they are not needed. We should be able to discern what sparks joy and what doesn't. If you do not like decorative objects in your house, dispose of them. Do not mistake your linger for joy.

## Does it still work?

Saving things that are broken, damaged, rusty, torn, outdated or not useful anymore is you saving clutter. If you do this, you need to stop before it becomes a habit. If it becomes a habit, your house could be a disaster before the year runs out. No matter how pretty they look or tempting it is to keep them, remember that they still don't serve their purpose. All they do is take up space and collect dust in the end.

## Is it a duplicate of something I have already?

It is pointless keeping too much of an item you have. You do not have to keep extra of things you already have. Keeping things like these is what led to that clutter from the start. Why would you want to keep something that takes up too much space in your home and makes you uncomfortable? It is not mandatory to have three or two of the same item.

If you have to choose between those four pairs of fancy stemware for family dinners, then it can't be that important having them around.

If you love having collections, be careful not to let them subtly turn to clutter. Do not stay oblivious to them. Search yourself and be sure if some of those collections are worth keeping.

## Am I saving it in case I might need it?

Holding on to things just in case you might need them is you holding on to clutter. Our blankets and fine china that we keep, because we hope to give them to our children as heirlooms can be also be the cause of clutter in our home.

Instead of hanging onto those things for 'what if' purposes, let them go and live your life freely.

## Was I aware that I had this item?

When you go through your stuff, and you see things that you didn't even notice or remember having, then that is clutter. If you have forgotten that you had some things with you, there's no need to keep them for keepsakes. Discard it!

## Do I have space for it?

If you don't have space for it, then it is clutter. There two sides to identifying this kind of clutter. You could have a big house with a lot of space, and yet, you may not have a home for some items. You could also have a small space for too many items that have a home. Tricky right?

However they are different. This is why it is important to be vigilant to clutter, especially in this form. If you have a small room for so many things, it does not mean that they should all be thrown away. What we can do is select those that have a home. If I have to decide between a trophy I was rewarded with at a job I never really liked and an apple slicer I use every weekend, what would it be? Obviously, I would choose to keep my apple slicer, because it has a home. It has a purpose, which makes it important to create space for.

If you have a big room for a lot of things, the temptation of accumulating them gets tougher to handle. You have to be critical about downsizing your possessions to only things that should or that already have homes. Anything that does not fit in your home is clutter. If you are pressed to create space for an item, then that item does not have a home and should not be left to remain a nuisance to your home.

**Would I replace it if it got lost in a fire or anywhere else?**

The tech gadgets we hold unto even when they get replaced should not be valued, because they are clutter in all shades.

**Do I like or love it?**

This is the most essential question of all. Every question all comes down to this. If you like or love it, that means you can create space for it. It implies that it is useful, valuable and not stored because of "what if" situations that'll most likely never happen. If such thing sparks joy or makes you happy, you should keep it. Otherwise, get rid of the clutter.

**(B). TAKE PICTURES**

Pictures help you change your perspective about what your home looks like with clutter around. You start to notice little details you never thought mattered before. When you take photos of your wardrobe, your room or your children's room, it places the imperfections at the background right before your eyes. The papers piled on the desk, the faded paints and the cords lying around the living room become more visible and help you focus on what to deal with clearly.

**(C). INVITE PEOPLE OVER**

Another way to find out places where clutter is hiding is to invite people over. Having company motivates you to fish out clutter you have been oblivious to. You would subconsciously be meticulous about the impression you want to give to your visitors.

**(D).** Go out to your friend's place or any other person's home and observe the structure their home takes. Is it neater than your house is? Are there things that you might need to take differently?

You could also go out for a vacation or take a short break from your home. Get a change of environment and come back home after. You'll start to realise that some things could just be there taking space and clustering your home.

**(E).** Stage your house like a curator. Examine your home with the mentality of a stranger who's just coming to your home for the first time. Take time to inspect and pick out the odd things around.

. . . . . . . .

Understanding the reasons you do the things you do is one of the most important steps to dealing with clutter. How? You get to know yourself better. You start making decisions that influence your personality type: like the problems you have overcoming, what motivates you and more. When you discover what ticks you off and what strikes a chord in you, each of these pre-decluttering steps become easier for you and you'll start to realise how everything just flows.

**It's my favorite day (2017). How to identify clutter in your home. Retrieved from**

https://www.itsmyfavoriteday.com/identify-clutter/

**Chrissy (2019). What is Clutter? The Meaning revealed (it may well surprise you). Retrieved from**

https://organisemyhouse.com/what-is-clutter/

**Home Storage Solutions 101 (n. d.). Decluttering Your Home (Series) Finding Your Path To Peace. Retrieved from**

https://www.home-storage-solutions-101.com/decluttering.html

# CHAPTER FOUR: THE JOURNEY TO MINIMALISM: DECLUTTERING 101

Decluttering is like exercising. You could admire your neighbor's house or even how this book seems to show you how easy decluttering works and how amazing your home could look when you start to declutter, jump right into the act and end up tired and frustrated at the thought that you may never hit your goal of living the ideal minimalist life. Very much like effective exercising, decluttering starts with a mindset. You must correct your attitude and perception of decluttering for yourself and by yourself. You should get ready to embrace a new and refreshing way of life.

Decluttering is only part of starting and sustaining life as a minimalist. It is a process towards minimalism. An amazing process, but it is not the goal. The goal is the happiness that living a life of minimalism brings. Decluttering is a big step towards this goal and that is what this book is about.

Decluttering goes beyond how your home gets the much-needed space; it goes to affect your whole life. Be ready to rewire your mind to what a minimalist life actually is and the huge benefits it accrues to you and those around you. It is a habit, not a project.

Decluttering is infinitely easier when you think of it as deciding what to keep, rather than deciding what to throw away.

But first, let's pull this term "minimalism" down to earth. It seems to have acquired a somewhat intimidating, elitist air, as it's often associated with chic, multimillion-dollar lofts with three pieces of furniture." Space! That's something we could all use more of! Space in our closets, space in our garages, space in our schedules, space to think, play, create, and have fun with our families…now that's the beauty of minimalism. It is a form of art that emphasizes extreme simplicity of form. It is actually more than art and fashionable conduct; it is living life in its true essence.

## MINIMALISM IS NOT

### A TIGHT CORNER; CHOOSING GOES OUT

While learning to declutter, you would have a feeling of helplessness. This is usual. You are actually the one taking charge at this stage of your life. You are not choosing what to lose, you are recognizing your sufficiency on your own and choosing what items to take along with you in your new life of true essence. And there is no pressure; it is the beginning of a lifestyle, so take your time. Over time, as you continue to declutter, you would realize that the thing that held so much value to you in your last declutter session would hold no value to you anymore. This happens when assessing our online shopping carts too. So, make your choice. What's staying?

## EMPTINESS

"Minimalism" conjures up images of spare, cool interiors, concrete floors, and gleaming white surfaces. It all sounds very sober, serious, and sterile. When placed against our "normal" bubbling lives, the word sounds so unreal. Most people hear the word "minimalism" and think "empty." But look at "empty" from another angle—think about what it is instead of what it is not —and now you have "space". Think on that.

## BORING; INSENSITIVITY

When we picture someone living a minimalist life, we usually picture a man in a near empty house with high apathy for social interaction, a boring life. On the contrary, minimalism helps your relationships. Minimalism helps you look past the material possessions of your friends and relate with them as they are. The process of decluttering will help you develop a sense of losing attachment to trivial things and placing them on more significant things such as memories and actual acts of gestures, making you value relationships even more. Of course, everyone knows where they are valued and love going there.

## BORNE OUT OF LACK

Minimalism is not borne out of lack. It is in fact an avenue to cash out of the rat race faster. Imagine how much money you would have stashed out for investment from not spending the money you would spend on buying unnecessary luxuries, paying for shipping, paying up on mortgages, replaying credit purchases, and making money for the insurance companies. The fact that minimalism is usually associated with emptiness makes matters worse, and it is unfortunate as "empty" is not altogether appealing, usually associated with loss, deprivation, and scarcity. Minimalism has nothing to do with that. It is simply shining light on what is truly needed to live as an individual and as one in relationship.

## **MINIMALISM IS:**

BEING IN CONTROL; CHOOSING WHAT STAYS

Minimalism is choosing what stays.

EQUITABLE

Decluttering creates a balance to your home, work place, and even your time. Most times, while decluttering and decluttering and decluttering and decluttering some more, we tend to not see any difference. The problem? Two things, you are decluttering and adding stuff and even more stuff, or you're decluttering the wrong way.

You can solve these problems by following a simple rule: if one comes in, one goes out. Every time a new item comes into your home, a similar item must leave. This rule works well for like items; say if one bag comes in, one bag goes out. However, if you have more shoes than bags, it would not be sensible to let a bag go out for a bag when there is excess shoes to let go of.

This rule does not apply all the time. You cannot expect to take out a "useless" item when buying a useless item. You take out the useless item and keep the "new" useless item out as well. Minimalism is balance.

SPACE

Minimalism not having an empty space but having space-now you have space. Yes, minimalism gives you SPACE! Something we could all use more of! Space in our closets, space in our schedules, space in our garages, space to think, live, play, create, and have more fun with our families. Oh, the beauty of minimalism. Becoming minimalists puts us in control of our stuff. We reclaim our space and restore function and potential to our homes and work life. We remake our houses into an open, airy, receptive hold for the substance of our lives. We declare independence from the tyranny of clutter. It is positively liberating and progressive!

FREEDOM AND CREATIVITY

Yes, decluttering makes you free. Being a minimalist makes you free and keeps you free. Imagine the stress that craving a single item gives you, from strolling through the mall to looking through the shelves for what you desire, to driving around town searching for the best store to shop from, to surfing the Internet comparing prices. In most cases, we want what we think we need yet we can't afford it at the moment. Will that discourage us? No. We scrape for money, empty our savings, put in more hours at work, and even take on more jobs to afford us money to get our "need".

In most cases, we easily charge it to our credit card and hope we can make the payments someday. Minimalism saves you that stress of seeking and gathering souvenirs. It gives you the time to enjoy every moment as it comes instead of spending time looking for what you think will remind you of the wonderful moment. Most times, this habit plunges us into the past and holds us back from making even more beautiful memories.

Not to be rigid, minimalism does not restrict you from keeping things that are dear to you. It simply shows you what truly is dear to you.

Let's see this analog of photographs of you and your family during a really fun vacation. Instead of having the pictures all over the place in a corner of your sitting room, decluttering is not saying you should have the pictures kept away in a box in the attic. That goes against the reason for the photographs, right? I mean these pictures are dear to you and every member of your family. Minimalism will suggest that you take all the photographs out of their frames and have all of them grouped into two or three bigger picture frames and placed against a wall. This creates more room and even more style to your home.

One question you can ask yourself in sorting out family photographs holding memories of a place is, "Do I cherish the fact that we've gone to this place or that Toby had his first walk during this trip?" If it is the former, you can keep just one photograph of all of you standing behind some place of significance where your family travelled. And if it is the latter, you can keep just that picture.

## FUN/MAXIMUM SATISFACTION

Minimalism is fun! The process of decluttering is fun as well.

However, laying this against what others consider fun, let's look at how fun is derived. Fun is basically being amused and entertained, and it is subjective. What would be fun for you would not be fun for me. In fact, minimalism helps you get the most fun. You might be thinking, "You've said so, but how?" Here's how and why. Looking at fun as entertainment and amusement, let's look at what entertainment is and why we need it.

Entertainment is usually meant to distract and make us feel like our lives are exciting. These come in the form of TV, movies, carnivals, going shopping, playing video games, eating, drinking, partying and even cleaning. Now, these each have other merits, but often they serve to distract us from work or other difficulties of life.

Unfortunately, this sort of fun is only a temporary high and often empty. And as soon as we're off that temporary high, we must find a new high from entertainment or else plunge back to our troubles. Sometimes, this trouble could include the thought of cleaning a house full of unnecessary stuff, cleaning over fifty dirty plates in a household of six, reorganizing the house after a party, etc.

Troubles you won't be having as a minimalist as you find contentment, and you don't need entertainment. That's not to say you'd never watch TV or good films or go to parties or theme parks ... but you would not need them for entertainment. You would not go shopping to fill an empty space in your life, to fill the need of finding happiness, because you're already content and don't have that empty space or need.

Finding contentment is learning to appreciate what you already have, learning the concept of having enough, learning to enjoy the simple things. It is not an overnight thing, but as you become more conscious of it, you'll find more contentment and need to be entertained, finding fun with whatever you really want to do, be it sleeping or taking a stroll.

## MINIMALISM IS MORE THAN JUST YOU

Something wonderful about minimalism is that your efforts at decluttering, reducing the product cycle of production, distribution and disposal, has a positive ripple effect in the world. Every time you decide against a frivolous purchase, every time you make do with something you have, borrow from a friend instead of buying, rearrange instead purchasing a classic, it's like giving a little gift to the planet (and the rest of its inhabitants). Cutting down on manufacturing activities, the water will be a little clearer, the forests a little fuller, the landfills a little emptier, air will be a little cleaner, saving the Earth from environmental harm. Not bad for wanting some clean space, right?

## WHY DO I NEED TO DECLUTTER FOR A MINIMALIST LIFESTYLE?

We unconsciously waste a lot of time chasing after unnecessary items on a whim without considering if they are actually needed. Decluttering to live the minimalist lifestyle helps our decision making, because we start thinking through before we purchase things. It checks our spending and prevents us from buying something that we may end up not liking later. Our self-control becomes predominant, and before you know it, you realize that you could literally restrict yourself to buying only necessary things without someone checking you or something.

**5.** It strengthens our ability to decide the items that are important to purchase on our scale of preferences. In the end, we become careful not to waste the money we worked hard for and save better.

5. Decluttering your home to achieve the minimalist lifestyle unleashes your authenticity. Most of us need to be reminded that there is more to ourselves than our outfits or the clothes we see on people. There are several people who do not have an identity. They live in the shadow of other people from how they dress to how they manage their homes. How does this happen? They create an artificial identity that is probably imposed by people around them or by what

they are told. It is ironic that it starts from our desire to be extravagant or sophisticated.

It's fine if you want to have that, but separate it from who you are. Ask yourself if that is what you really want. Minimalism seems trivial, but it is really key. It makes you desire to be real with who you are without being overly influenced by the opinion of other people. It suppresses insecurity.

Staying true to yourself with minimalism means that you know what you stand for, and no one's negativity can easily change you. If I wear a simple black dress that I like, no one can randomly laugh at me and change my opinion about my dress. Why? I am aware that my personality is supposed to be the center of attraction- not the dress, not the person who made the comment, but my choice and my comfort.

10. Minimalism also portrays power. When you wear a minimalist attire or make a minimalist decision, you have the power to control what others think about you, purely based on you as a person. No one can jump into any conclusion when you give them no clue or reason to do so.

- It saves time. Reducing your possession helps you access your things more easily and quickly. You would not have to waste time hunting for clothes or a necklace in the midst of so many things. You literally save space from owning less. Your space before easier and quicker to take care of in the long term. Minimalism helps you set your priorities right. Instead of thriving on materialistic objects, you get to have more time for your studies, your career, your family and more. You get to thrive on happiness and life in general. It gives you more time to meditate and follow your desires.

- It clears your mental space. When your living space is cleaner and tidier, your mind tends to be less cluttered. A minimalistic approach can be transcending to the spirit and our health. Clutter should be avoided and our lives should not be so burdened with junk.

Imagine taking time to deal responsibly with the clutter in your room for a day. It makes you feel like you accomplished something. Clearing your physical space clears your mental space, if you let it. Decluttering your wardrobe to simplicity gives this feeling of enrichment, contentment, and freedom. Think of it as the retail therapy you go through, when you need to feel good about yourself or when you need closure.

With minimalism, you feel like you are personally evolving in the positive light. It focuses on you being a better version of yourself. The moment you take decluttering as key for you, you feel light and free from surrounding yourself with unnecessary items that you did not need to attach yourself with from the start. You begin to place more importance on your experiences with people and values rather than material possessions and places.

Surrounding yourself with items you love and displaying only the items most valuable to you will make you feel happier. You won't have to search through lots of items that you don't like. Favorite items won't get lost at the back of the cupboard or the bottom of the drawer. You would only use the things you love and your life would be filled with more happiness as a result.

Last year, I went through a survey that focused on bloggers and their principles about minimalism. There was a particular principle that I held to my heart, the principle of "unobtrusive beauty". The principle is built on the belief that it is hard to go wrong with simplicity.

Clothes with **"clashing prints and bright colors can be tiring, but simplicity is optically soothing...because in simple pieces of fabric, beaut lies and someway manage to draw the attention to the completeness of the while appearance, where for instance, print or very bright colors can distract from the overall presentation and make it look off balance by putting emphasis** on just parts of your look when the beauty in a look actually lies in the outfit as a whole."

## WHAT ARE THE METHODS OF DECLUTTERING?

### 1. The Kon Mari Method

The Kon Mari method is one of the most popular decluttering methods out there. It gained a lot of attention through the book, *The Changing Magic Tidying Up* by Marie Kondo.

Basically, the principle of the Kon Mari method entails you choosing what to keep and then decluttering the rest all at once. Most methods follow the room by room order of organisation. The Kon Mari only follows this particular sequence: clothes, then books, followed by documents, miscellaneous (e.g., kitchen), and finally sentimental items. Marie Kondo, the decluttering expert, advocates the philosophy that each possession has a place, and you should know exactly where to find everything. This is only possible if you reduce the amount of your material items.

It is sort of exceptional, because you are not pressured to get rid of items first. Hence, your difficulty to let them go reduces. Instead, you just pick the ones that are dear to you and throw the rest away.

You could start by collecting every single item you own in a particular category and putting them in a big pile. For instance, get every top that you own and put them on the bed. Hold or feel the items and decide which ones you want to keep. You could even wear them to be very sure about which tops your heart has a soft spot for. Ask yourself if they spark joy each time you feel or wear them. After putting them away, thank those items for the pleasure they brought to your life throughout the time they were with you. Then, you can donate them, sell or give them to someone else who deserves it.

Marie Kondo's approach to minimalism through decluttering changes one's perspective about clothes they never thought they had relationships with. It is really practical.

## 2. The Closet Hanger Method

The closet hanger method became very well-known after Oprah mentioned it as a pretty good method to use if you are trying to figure out what you want to declutter. Just like the name, it works when you have your clothing stored on hangers in your wardrobe. When you want to use this method, it is important that you make sure all your hangers are facing the same direction. Whenever you wear one, out it into a reverse position, so you can identify which ones you wore and the ones you have not worn. That way, you can track exactly what has been used, a few pieces at a time. After some time (six months or a year), you can choose to get rid of the clothes that still remained in the same direction (those clothes you did not wear).

**3. The Minimalist Game**

Another method you can use for decluttering is the minimalist game. It turns the decluttering experience into a fun game on social media. Hundreds of people play it using the #minsgame hashtag on social media every month. The game works like this: as each day of the month passes, the number of things you unclutter increases. So, if it is the first day of the month, you remove one item. On the second one day, you remove two items, and it goes on through the rest of the month.

The game requires consistency, so if you feel that it is not enough to follow the trend on social media, you could play it with your family, friends or colleagues. That way, you can all check how constant you are with it.

On the other hand, if you feel like it is unnecessary to involve other people in your personal resolutions, you could set up things to help you follow through with the game. I'm talking about setting up a minimalist game calendar or organizing reminders in the form of post-it notes for yourself. You could do them on your phone too for easy access.

## 4. Three OR Four Box Method

When it comes to dealing with clutter in your home, the three/four box method is more flexible and straightforward than other methods. You can unclutter for as long as you want or at your convenience. Here, you sort the clutter into three or four categories by setting up boxes. Label them and decide on what you want to do with each of them. You label them as:

* Keep

* Give away/Sell

* Throw away, and

* Undecided

**OR**

* "Love" box (the ones you love and intend to keep)

* "Maybe" box (the ones you are unsure about getting rid of)

* "Nope" box (the ones you would totally discard from the house), and

* "Seasonal" box (the ones that are only useful in seasons)

Either way, pick up the clutter, separate it into the boxes and act on them according to their names.

## 5. One In, One Out Method

This method is similar to the "three or four box method". It is flexible, and it involves simply giving away one thing every day for a particular period of time. It could be one bag each day or any other thing. The one in, one out method builds your habit of decluttering. It could simply transform your home by reducing stuff each day.

## 6. Packing Party

This method is awesome if you are moving to your new place. It takes a lot of time and effort and is very effective. All you have to do is invite some friends over and pack all your stuff into the boxes as if you are moving. For the next few months, bring out only what you use frequently or what you need to use, instead of unpacking everything right away. The remaining things left inside the boxes after four months should be discarded. Your friends, the packing party, would help you discard those items.

**7. To-do List/Checklist**

If none of those methods work for you, you could make a list of places in your room that you would want to declutter. To get started, begin with the easiest down to the most difficult or vice versa- according to your choice and your schedule.

There are times that I create a 30-day Decluttering to-do list in this format:

## *CHECKLIST*

11. Declutter 3 things from the fridge- whether from the top, the front or the side of the fridge
12. Declutter 3 items from the pantry
13. Declutter 3 things from the kitchen sink
14. Declutter 3 items from the living room
15. Declutter 3 items from the dining room
16. Declutter 3 things from my wardrobe
17. Declutter 3 things from the book shelf
18. Declutter 3 things from my dresser top

19. Declutter 3 items of clothing (socks, underwear, outfits)
20. Declutter 3 pieces of jewelry
21. Declutter 3 items from my makeup drawer
22. Declutter 3 unused toiletries (lotions, soaps, shampoos)
23. Declutter 3 items from the laundry room
24. Declutter 3 items from my bathroom/toilet
25. Declutter 3 items from the car

If you prefer the to-do list method, you could modify it to your own interest. You could increase the number of items you would be decluttering or reduce the number of days you want to have your challenge. The important part is that you follow it well.

## 8. 12-12-12 Challenge

All you have to do is locate 12 items you want to throw away, 12 items to donate, and 12 items that should be placed in the right location. Before you know it, you would have successfully organised 36 items in your home.

## 9. Project 333 Experiment

Courtney Carver invented this minimalist experiment with numbers to challenge people to wear only 33 items for 3 months. It is a pretty engaging method. The experiment centers on choosing your signature style for all 33 items; that would include articles of clothing, jewelry, shoes and other clothing accessories. Then, you choose these 33 items and pack up the rest of your items out of plain sight. The Project 333 method is not just for people to be challenged. It is also a platform where people connect by sharing their experiences after trying it out and getting answers to things they are curious about.

**10.** Have a donation budget annually. Then complement it with giving away your things to charity, instead of money.

**11.** There are different decluttering methods also recommended on the basis of your personality type.

Whichever method works out for you, the important thing is to challenge yourself to live with less and see what you learn from the experience.

Learn to change your perspective too. Minimalism offers a powerful approach to decluttering with a number of strategies to help you change your perspective and begin to notice some clutter you may have missed. Use your imagination. Psychology today certifies the use of your imagination to help declutter objects that may seem difficult to remove. Try asking yourself unique questions like, "If I was buying this now, how much would I pay?"

Always stay open-minded and think of ideas to improve your home like taking photos of your house, inviting a toddler over, or asking your co-worker or boss to meet in your office. The idea is to cause you to see your home in a new light.

However, if all these methods are not working out for you, reach out to experts. You can also hire a professional decluttered or professional organizer to come do the work for you.

At this point, I would like to end by quoting some of my favorite minimalist bloggers:

**"Removing clutter makes room for a life focused on the things that matter most. It opens up physical space in our home and mental space in our mind."**

— Joshua Becker & Brian Gardner

"You'd be surprised at the results that come from committing to just ten minutes a day of decluttering and organizing."

— Peter Walsh

"Decluttering is ultimately about alignment. It spurs greater congruence between our values and our actions…Before any of us can minimize our homes and lives, we must be convinced the lifestyle we want is worth our effort…Before you remove even one item from your home, I encourage you to sit down and articulate one or more reasons why you want to declutter your home."

— Joshua Becker

**Francine Jay (2010). The Joy of Less, A Minimalist Living Guide: How to Declutter, Organise, and Simplify Your Life.**

**Erin L.Murphy (2018). Less Is More Work: A Govermentality Analysis Within Minimalism Discourse.**

# CHAPTER FIVE : FIVE MINUTES!!!

You are starting to realize the clutter around you now, and it all starts to come into shape. The thought of having a clutter-free home is so life-giving. You could literally picture that perfect image in your mind, and it feels so calm and peaceful. But, the thought of organising the clutter in the entire house seems impossible. There is probably so much work slowly piling up or little things unconsciously eating into our free time during the weekends. This week, you stay up watching your favorite TV series and procrastinate dealing with the clutter. Next week, you are taking care of the children when they suddenly get sick. And it's one other little thing or the other taking over your weekends unconsciously.

Cleaning the entire house with these unpredictable routines would actually be unreasonable, but devoting a few minutes to reduce the clutter with small steps should not be too much. With 5 minutes, you could be in the right direction to decluttering your home. It would help you a great deal if you start with the minimalist approach to declutter. How? Minimize the clutter by taking care of some specific spots gradually, until you touch every place in your home. If you think five minutes is too small to take care of the clutter one step at a time, you may have to rethink that. Five minutes could get a lot done if you use the time prudently and quickly. It could work for any one, regardless of your living arrangement. All you need to do is begin decluttering your go-to places or the most frequently used spots in your home.

It could be those five minutes while you wait for your family to get prepared for thanksgiving dinner. It could be those five minutes you spend on your phone before you go to work. You could spend those five minutes cleaning your makeup bag, your purse or your underwear drawer. The five-minute deal is a life saver! You can help your child clean out her backpack or arrange your hangers in the closet. You could check through your child's (children's) bookcase and pull out all the old board books she has outgrown or pull all the winter coats out of the closet to create room for summer jackets. Using five minutes each day could really help.

When you complete small tasks like this, you will definitely accomplish that perfect image in your mind of what your home deserves to look like- peaceful, calm and free. In fact, you will be happy that you did.

However, if you are confused about where to begin, here are few different small tasks that you could carry out in your home:

# I. DECLUTTER YOUR KITCHEN

One of the many things that fill people's homes are duplicate kitchen accessories. I am talking about excess plates, cups, mugs, bowls and bottles accumulating in the cupboards in our kitchen, the fridge, the pantry, and every other place in the kitchen. We need to be practical and ask ourselves how many of them we and our families make use of.

Make a decision today to declutter every duplicate item in your kitchen. You could take five minutes whenever you can and start anywhere. It could be five/ten items getting uncluttered from the front, side, and top of the fridge this weekend. Next weekend, it could be you wiping the fridge clean. It doesn't have to be on the weekend. If you have some free time during the week, create time to get your valuable kitchen space. Whichever way you start, it is always more simple, easy and fun to do when you make a list.

Here's a sample:

**To-do list for decluttering my kitchen**

- Wash and dry the cutlery
- Clean the kitchen sink
- Unload the dishwasher
- Put dishes in the dishwasher

- Declutter 5/10 items in the cupboard (cups, containers, plates, etc.)
- Declutter reusable containers and/or lids
- Wipe the stove clean (the knobs and the stovetop)
- Clean the oven
- Remove expired items from the fridge
- Wipe clean the top of the fridge
- Wipe clean the front of the fridge
- Wipe clean the side of the fridge
- Declutter 5/10 things from the top of the fridge
- Declutter 5/10 things from the front of the fridge
- Declutter 5/10 things from the side of the fridge
- Declutter 5/10 items from the pantry
- Wipe the cabinets
- Sweep the kitchen
- Empty the kitchen trash
- Get rid of expired/unused spices

## II. CLEAN YOUR VEHICLE/CAR

Another common place where we harbor clutter is our vehicles. A lot of times we fill our cars with unnecessary things, especially those old CDs we keep as our supposed collection. If it isn't the CDs, it's the several receipts we got from the convenience store or the stray toys our kids leave about in the car, abandoned water bottles, coins or more paper clutter.

Instead of breeding all of this clutter in your vehicle, take some bags to the car and purge them all. Decide what you want to throw away as garbage and what you want to relocate or give away. After you fill these bags and free your car of the unneeded clutter, you will be surprised by how much relief you feel.

## III. DECLUTTER THE DREADED DRAWER

We all have that one or two drawers that we are afraid of tackling, because it reeks of so much junk. Yet, we hold on to it because we feel in between all of that junk, there will definitely be important items we may need later. Some drawers may take more than five minutes to clean, but there is no reason for you not to make it a five-minute task. Instead of exaggerating how long it will take to clean them, start somewhere. Try clearing at least half the clutter there first within the time frame you set and see how fast you can achieve this when you put your mind to it.

## IV. CLEAR OUT THAT PAPER CLUTTER

Paper clutter literally takes half the storage spaces or even more in several households. We may not be conscious of how much clutter those magazines, old newspapers, mail, handouts and other stack of papers are creating in our homes. But, we need to stay on top of the clutter and control what comes in, what stays, and what goes.

There's one thing we need to keep in mind too. If we are decluttering our mail, that should include our e-mails too. I know this does not fall into the 'paper clutter' category, but it is clear that we possibly regard it as a blind spot. Our e-mails should be organised by folders and not in clusters.

That being said, the first thing to do while dealing with paper clutter is to look through the papers piling up in the wrong places (coffee tables, home office desks, kitchen counters, dining room). After sorting them out, move on to larger piles and purge them ruthlessly.

You could take another five minutes the next time for creating clutter checkers. For instance, you could create a basket for your mail and an alphabetical filing system, pending the time that you sort them out.

With that, you can sort the mail immediately, effortlessly pay your bills online, and toss junk, old magazines or catalogs into recycling. With your five-minute project, you are basically unstoppable! Stay eco-friendly by putting up a container for paper recycling, in order to avoid junk mail that is uncalled for.

## V. SORT THE BEDROOM DRESSER

Joshua Becker says, "Bedrooms should promote rest, relaxation and intimacy- not upheaval and unrest." Think about it. You come back from work or a really stressful day with the kids. You are so drained, you just want to rest in the bedroom without being disturbed or with no interference. Which view is better- going to sleep with a peaceful atmosphere and spacious setting or going to sleep in the bedroom with tons of paper and clothes? I think it's pretty obvious.

We all want to go to sleep in a bedroom that gives us a calm feeling. Do you notice that when you sleep and wake up sometimes, you feel like you didn't even sleep well at all? It's like your energy got sapped double time- probably worse than when you went to sleep. Some other time, it could be your whole mood changing.

Eighty percent of the time, I can bet the clutter on your bedroom dresser contributes to that whole funny feeling. You think I could be wrong? Try it. Take up a challenge to clear the top of your bedroom dresser in five minutes. Notice how your mood changes and you feel more refreshed and calm.

## VI. DECLUTTER THE FRIDGE/REFRIGERATOR

It could be so satisfying to have your refrigerator filled with varieties you bought from the grocery store. But the bad side is that there is a slight tendency for those items to proliferate the refrigerator at some point. Our fridges should be tidy- if not always, at least, most of the time. Take a strict five minutes to examine what's in there. After looking through, you should be able to determine what needs to be used up in tonight's dinner or tomorrow's breakfast. Get rid of bad leftovers and make it a habit to check your fridge regularly. You could even imbibe a zero-waste culture to avoid food wastage and any subtle food clutter later.

## VII. CLEAN THE BATHROOM

Reduce the bathroom clutter regularly and avoid buying new shampoo when you've not finished the previous one. Remember, decluttering as a minimalist also means disciplining yourself to be contented. Mildly clean sensitive parts of the bathroom to make the bathroom easier to clean later. Check through and transfer those items you hardly use in the bathroom to the cabinet or anywhere else apart from the shower. If you observe that you don't miss them or still use them after some time, put them away. You won't regret it.

Dispose the empty containers of skin care contents and cosmetics, overused hair accessories, the old medicines and expired products that are accumulating in the medicine chest in the bathroom in a few minutes. While you are at it, dispose of them properly.

## VIII. TACKLE THOSE STRAY TOYS

Having toys around the house should not be new to you if you have a child or young children in your home. It can be overwhelming dealing with all these toys scattered around the house and trying to get it together in your life. Don't worry. I got your back, which is why we will be talking about decluttering your home as a parent in next chapters.

But in the meantime, return those toys to where they belong. It's advisable you do that when they all go to bed or when they get distracted. Pick toys that they've outgrown and place them in a bag that you'll give out for donations later.

You could also set a no-clutter policy for your children to abide. Better still, if you think the toys around the house are getting too much, how about you consider living with less- the minimalist style?

## IX. CLEAR OUT YOUR GARAGE

If there's any place that gets accumulated with clutter the fastest, I think it's the garage. We dump random stuff we do not need in the middle of the garage until there's no space to even park our cars. Instead of waiting until we start tripping and falling over things, start a five-minute project to organize the garage in bits! As you declutter parts of the garage, organize them too. Make sure those items all have a home, so your efforts won't go to waste.

. . . . . . . .

There are so many places in your home that you could apply the strict five-minute rule for easy decluttering. There's the living room, the dining room, some parts of your kid's drawer, the laundry, your kid's stroller, the couches, the bookshelf and so on. You could create shortcuts to dealing with your clutter in five minutes. You could set baskets in the bathroom and kitchen to control potential clutter, wipes and cleaning supplies in every room and more. By the time you engage in five-minute tasks for about a week, you would have cleared about an hour or two worth of decluttering. Take it upon yourself to accomplish a five-minute project today and see how much better you feel.

**Joshua Becker (2017). Seven 5-Minutes Decluttering Projects You Can Accomplish Today. Retrieved from**

https://www.becomingminimalist.com/5-minute-decluttering-projects/

Elizabeth Larson (2019). 15-Minutes Clutter Sweeps for Every Room in Your Home. Retrieved from

https://www.thespruce.com/quick-clutter-sweeps-for-every-room-2647982

Kelly (2014). How To Declutter Your House In Five Minutes-16 Quick Ways. Retrieved from

https://redefinedmom.com/how-to-declutter-your-house-in-five-minutes/

Katherine Martino (2017). Take 5 minutes to declutter these key spots in your home. Retrieved from

https://www.treehugger.com/cleaning-organizing/amp/take-5-minutes-to-delutter-these-key-spots-in-your-home.html

# CHAPTER SIX: DELUTTERING AS A FASHION-LOVING MINIMALIST

Every one of us has a fashion statement. Your fashion statement is your personal style. Our fashion statement is spoken in the way we express ourselves through our clothes or clothing accessories. You may think you are not the fashionable type, but your supposed numbness to fashion is your own fashion statement too.

We basically define who we are by our fashion statements. No wonder why it seems easy at times to judge what kind of personality a person would have just by the way they look. The fashion statement of one person differs from another, and it can be hard finding their similarities rather than finding their differences. But do you know the most common similarity we share in our fashion statements? The opinion that "more" means "safer" and "trendy".

We love the idea of having more- more heels, more bags, more discount coupons from our favorite fashion store, more of those limited editions we fear may become scarce or sold out quickly, more shopping sprees, and more of all the other things we love. So, when we hear about decluttering or minimalism, it gives us that tingly feeling that makes us uncomfortable. But guess what? It is not what you think it is.

Decluttering those clothes to achieve the minimalist lifestyle is not washing your fashion statement down the drain. You can be a minimalist and still look chic. The Minimalist Fashion style is not made up of those cold, lifeless shades of black and white pieces you imagine. It is not boring; in fact, minimalist fashion is all about the beauty in simplicity. There is no restriction to what it should be like. It is just about choosing quality over quantity- which makes it more sustainable. It is about eliminating the unnecessary stuff and focusing on the essentials. In the end, you get to save more money, time, morale, and energy.

Did you know that minimalism is increasingly becoming a renowned fashion lifestyle around the world today? Even some of the most successful and popular people seemingly practice it too. Fashion figures like Grace Codington, Vera Wang, Karl Lagerfeld and Michael Kors favor the minimalist approach to fashion. Also, Mark Zuckerberg and even former President Obama both have a thing for wearing the same colors constantly. If you didn't know, well now you do.

You see, the whole point of taking the minimalist approach to fashion is not to reduce your clothes to very small amounts like five or four pieces of clothing. It focuses on your attitude to your clothes-changing from being ignorant to being self-aware. You transit from being carefree to being intentional about what clothes or accessories should stay or be reduced in your home.

Come to think of it. How many of the clothes in your wardrobe do you wear in a year? Why do you get confused most of the time about what to wear? It's probably because you have too much stuff you do not need. Don't you think it would do you and your closet a lot of good if you choose to disarm some of them today? Would you rather wake and open your closet in a frenzy about what to wear or would you rather wake up and open your closet confident and happy with the things you only love and need?

Now that you have thought of it, you want the best, right? You want to wake up without getting less confident about what to choose from, without stressing yourself. But how is that possible? You can achieve that minimalist wardrobe with three steps.

**Step One: DECLUTTERING WITH INTENTION(S)**

The first thing to do is declutter. The truth is you can't deal with your clutter or stay true to your fashion statement if you do not declutter. It is important that you declutter with a reasonable intention. Only then can you move on to the next step.

Again, I repeat, please declutter intentionally. Do not declutter if you do not have any purposeful reason for doing it. Being intentional means being conscious of what you consume in terms of material things. How do you know your intention for decluttering? Think about your daily needs. Take note of the current state of your closet and what items are in it.

To nurture a sustainable fashion statement for ourselves, we need to ask who we are, where we live, what we engage in, what the things we need and want are, and what our goals are. Be practical about your lifestyle. Decluttering is a thought process. When you are able to answer these questions practically, deciding on what or how to declutter would get easier.

For instance, if your job requires you to dress formally for six days of the week, you should not be concerned about discarding items for formal occasions. You should not be keeping more casual wear than normal.

If you stay where the weather is frequently chilly, you should not be tossing away most of your sweaters, scarves, gloves or mufflers. Your bum shorts or short gowns may not be that useful. Only a few would do.

Are you more of the reserved type that prefers to watch a movie at home rather than go for parties? Rid yourself of those excessive heels that you don't use before they eat up your personal space.

Discover innovative ways to get rid of your clothes. You could simply apply any of the methods of decluttering, like the three/four box method or the Project 333 that was stated in one of the previous chapters.

But if you think some of those stilettos might still be useful for special occasions, you could keep a few of them. If you also think you may not actually be ready to throw those matching tops your ex got into the bin, you could keep them until you get over them. Like Marie Kondo would say, the purpose of decluttering in the first place is to remove the things that don't "spark joy" in you anymore. You must be sure that the clothes you leave in your wardrobe after decluttering are clothes that make you happier each time you wear it. Staying on top of this will help you reflect on where you stand in identifying yourself through your personal style, what you are missing, and the changes you need to make in the future.

**Step Two: Generate your style**

The next thing to do after decluttering, is to come to terms with what your style is. What kind of patterns or designs do you like in your clothes, shoes or jewelry? I said earlier that everyone has a fashion statement. Not everyone knows theirs, but we all have one, whether we're aware of it or not. Most of the time, when our closets get cluttered, it may be because we do not have any knowledge of what our style is.

Meanwhile, it might be slightly difficult getting a hold of that at this period of time, because you may just be getting used to having a wardrobe with fewer things in it. So, you don't have to be in a rush to realize what your fashion style is. Take your time. As you take your time, appreciate your efforts at taking a step towards achieving that dream wardrobe you wanted. You will start to admire those items you love in your closet.

After a while, observe the clothes you took out of the clutter you got rid of. I mean, those clothes you chose to keep because you liked the feeling they gave you when you wore them. Do they have lots of bold prints in them or flowery fabrics? Are they lean towards the sweatshirts, casual tops and shorts or the shirts and gowns? Do they fall under the neutral colors or are they flashy? Whichever one it is, you should go for those styles that you identify yourself with more.

People often make the mistake of choosing the minimalist lifestyle and the minimalist aesthetic. If you are choosing the minimalist lifestyle, then you are choosing to live strictly with less clothes, less accessories, less colors. If you are choosing minimalist aesthetic, then we are talking about living with less but in a more liberal manner. That is, minimal clothes with minimal color scheme. It could be a combination of black, white and grey colors with some shades of red or red and blue.

Do you still have no clue about what your personal fashion statement might be? Aside from taking note of the designs that you are attached to in your wardrobe, here are some creative ways that could help you:

Turn your ideal or imaginary fashion look into reality by checking out styles that look fabulous to you. Check for styles and save them on your device. They could be jewelry choices, shoes, shades, make overs and so on. Chances are, your saved styles embody what your personal style is. And so, it will trigger a hint on what your fashion statement looks like. Once you find out what your vibe is, you'll definitely want to stick to it.


One of the most effective medium to use is Pinterest. Create a board where you can save designs or pin styles that you like. Then, go back to them and examine if they look edgy, uptown, classic or something else that's entirely different. In case you don't really flow with Pinterest, there are apps solely designed for you to do that.

Color palettes! Perform some color tests to find out how you want your personal style to improve with the minimalist approach. Find a color palette that works for you. It all comes down to choosing a color mix that suits you, as long as they are not too intense in color. If choosing all black makes you feel badass, then go for it. If you want a combination of neutral colors with a gentle mix of a flashy color, go for it too. Just do you and be consistent with it.

## Step Three: IMBIBE THE MINIMALIST FASHION CULTURE

One of the greatest gift minimalism gives you is the drive to step out of your comfort zone. The minimalist fashion culture changes your notion about material things subconsciously. It's like killing three birds with one stone (Yes I said three, not two). What gives?

First, you get to purge yourself, your fashion statement, and your home of the unhealthy clutter.

Second, you get to identify who you really are by identifying your own style. Your opinion about fashion changes subconsciously. You'll start to realize that less is really more.

Third, you unleash that creative side you perhaps never knew existed in you. Your experiments with colors gives you an insight on what stylist technique would suit your lifestyle. Recreate styles you love in the most beautiful, yet simple way. With minimalism, you tend to pay more attention to detail in your clothing and think outside the box.

## MINIMALIST STYLING TIPS

1. Streamline what you buy

Streamlining the things to buy after organizing your closet may be very hard to do, but trust me, it will save you the trouble of making a mess of your closet again and going back to square one.

When deciding what to buy, start with the basics: do they fit your color palette or styling technique? Will it be useful for me in the long run? Do I have something similar? Is it unavoidable? Should I really buy it? Will it be expensive to maintain? Am I buying it because it's pretty rather than buying it because it is durable and versatile? Is it really of high-quality?

If you answer these basic questions with an intentional mindset, you should be able to determine what you should buy and what you shouldn't. Ensure that those items only spark joy (joy, not happiness, because joy is long-term and happiness is short-term), fit your routine, and suit your idea of what beauty is.

2. Develop a Capsule/Capsule-ish wardrobe

Capsule wardrobes are like the conservative versions of minimalist wardrobes. It entails having an extremely fewer number of clothes, compared to the minimalist wardrobe- with stern concentration on quality and versatility of clothes. If you're developing your wardrobe into a capsule wardrobe, it takes a lot of determination and planning. For instance, you might have to cut your spending severely and resolve not to buy anything for a whole season. Pretty rigid, right? Even so, it works well for some people. You would have to focus on what to prioritize in your outfits, and separate them from what you don't need that badly. There's a limit to what you can have.

If you're trying to manage the other things to make up for your closet, capsule wardrobes would work better for you. It solely works to achieve a special purpose. For instance, if you want to create a wardrobe for your seasonal wear only, you could use the capsule wardrobe. All you need to do is put in about five of those seasonal pieces or less.

But, it doesn't have to involve you strictly following it. It's really not so much of a one-way traffic. You can develop a capsule-ish wardrobe. I mean, building up a wardrobe that falls between the minimalist and capsule wardrobes. In the same measure, you could develop your capsule-ish wardrobe to lean on the principle of the minimalist wardrobe instead. Employing the minimalist wardrobe principle means your shopping parameter is lenient.

Both principles have their advantages and disadvantages, but the end process is the same- you get to have the wardrobe you cherish. That is, a reduced number of items for diverse purposes. The main thing is that you learn how to invest in pieces that are well made, sustainable and fashionable for you. You get to prove how much you can come up with, even when your clothes are downsized.


3. Adopt those regular patterns that your outfit tends to follow. I mean those go-to outfits that comes to your mind when you think of outfits that you could easily wear. It could be those ankle boots and signature ornaments you love or those tightly fitted skirts that pop up in your head when you think of what wear. If they keep coming up, adopt them and turn them to your signature style.

4. Follow minimalist blogs and brands to develop your fashion statement. If going to the fashion store you love is too tempting for you to do your shopping, make it a habit to follow minimalist blogs and brands, so you could get a source of inspiration to build yourself up in the minimalist approach to fashion. Keeping up on such blogs and buying from such brands will push away that urge to breed clutter later.

Minimalist bloggers and brands emphasize Ethical fashion and the High-quality of clothes too. Following up on them would simply restrain your nudge towards buying or having more than you need. Examples of some renewed minimalist brands and blogs include; FIGNTY, All Things Lovely, Mijeong Park, VETTA, Helmut Lang, Lunya, A. P. C., All Things Fatima, The Undone, Gentry Portofino, Magali Pascal, COS, Aesthetic Lines, Calivintage, FRAME and Echo+Air.

5. Try fashion experiments

As you begin your journey to a minimalist lifestyle, you need to keep moving forward. Don't stop decluttering and don't stop experimenting on what exactly generates your style. Upgrade your fashion statement always. This does not have to be mandatory though. If you are not a fan of change, and you are really comfortable with what you already have, you could stick to it. Just make sure your style keeps reflecting that dream wardrobe you love.

6. Manage your accessories properly

Although most of us probably prefer not to sort out our jewelry and other accessories, it is crucial that we declutter them. They are part of our fashion statement, and so, as unpleasant as the thought of minimizing them may seem, we need to reduce our accessories to the things we love for the benefit of our closets and our lives.

**Logan Payne (2017). What is Minimalist Style? Retrieved from http:// stitchfix.com**

**Sarah Anne Hayes (n. d.). A Definitive Guide to Minimalist Fashion. Retrieved from http://nosidebar.com**

**Dan Silvester (n. d.). The Minimalist Wardrobe: How to Love All Your Clothes. Retrieved from http://www.dansilvestre.com**

**Maria Sensed (2015). Less is More: How to Build a Chic Minimalist Wardrobe in 4 Steps. Retrieved from http://the fashionspot.com**

**Dr Amber Martin-Woodhead (n.d.). Minimalism as sustainable fashion.**

# *CHAPTER SEVEN:* DELUTTERING AND RELATIONSHIPS 1: Decluttering with your family and friends IN THE minimalist APPROACH

Having a family is one of the best things that could happen to a person. You learn how to compromise, set your priorities, love unconditionally and appreciate the imperfections and values of your partner and children- and every other member of the family. Regardless of our differences, we just want to spend memorable time with them and be there for them always. It is such a deep sensation of so many beautiful emotions all at once.

Nonetheless, as time passes, our responsibilities and the usual activities that we go through without sweat become surprisingly arduous. We go through transition with getting stuff for the new baby, moving to a new house, new work opportunities and more. Suddenly, there's really no time to deal with things we own in our own homes. Then, the inevitable clutter comes around, and everyone gets affected by it. In the midst of these complications, all we just want to do is go back to the way our family was before-calm, simple and clutter-free.

You see, minimalism focuses on beauty in simplicity. It concentrates on our freedom to be all of what we desire as a family and more. Yet, it has different meanings to us, because we interpret it differently. Describing minimalism may be technical, but one thing is for sure-the benefits are all the same. Adopting Minimalism opens you up to positively new ideas and new ways of living. It changes our lives.

Truth be told, minimalism is not as easy as it is believed to be. It is not some magical transformation that happens overnight. It requires lots of sacrifices and discipline, especially when you're trying to imbibe the culture of living with less with your family. Still, the benefits outweigh the process. When you start decluttering with the minimalist approach as a family, you will see the worth of it sooner than you expected.

Minimalism saves you time- I mean a lot of time. It's funny how we don't really recognise the value of time that we spend with our families, until our children grow up and we retire. Decluttering projects give you less stress and fewer things to organise. Due to that, you spend valuable time with your family and experience meaningful memories. There's enough time for vacations and recreating family time. A vivid illustration is watching less TV.

Rather than pay for TV that everyone can hardly watch, you can save money and invest in family-oriented TV shows that can be watched together.

Decluttering your house to live with less does not bring you some enchantment that makes you happy all of a sudden. It is the choice and decisions that it emphasises. What decisions would make you happier? Saving time to go to the gym? Balancing your full-time job with spending time with your family to make home-made recipes on the weekend? More energy is saved too. You become intentional about how you use your time. It teaches you to be productive.

Minimalism makes you conscious of your environment. For instance, instead of buying more plastic products, we find ourselves leaning towards healthier options of recycling and using any other method that prevents us from being wasteful. Minimalism focuses on creating an eco-friendly environment that would be safe for you and your family.

Owning less helps you become a better parent and spouse. The current society lives for the theory of excessive consumerism. Excess money, excess toys, excess trendy outfits, excess need for safety and so much more. There's virtually no end to it, and it gets so overwhelming and burdensome to survive with. So, all our values as a family end up in disorder. When we only keep possessions that spark true joy in your family, the values that hold up our families stay on track.

Minimalism teaches you to be content, not just with material things, but also with your principles, your flaws, your inner peace and your happiness. The tendency to depend on possessions and people to make us happy will slowly change. You just lose that the feeling you get when you look inferior or sad about people dressing more flamboyantly than you. Why? Because you begin to love yourself and look at things deeper than their face value. You realise that trying to follow the latest trends and searching for the most jaw-dropping gifts, only because that's what we see around us is not serving us. When you become aware of this, you become a source of inspiration to your family and a source that reminds them to reflect and live in the minimalist lifestyle.

**Minimalist Lifestyle Tips for decluttering with your family**

How do we manage the clutter that our families contribute to?

**1). Curtail clutter by category/type: your family's clothing, shoes, kitchen utensils and miscellaneous items**

Deal with those clothes, dishes, and other random items by paring them down to only the necessary ones that your family needs. If a large number of things are available around the house, they should be in use, not just lying around. Tackle them at the absence of your family, so you won't be reconsidering keeping them.

You could pick out those unused clothes in the drawer for donation while doing the laundry. Cut down the dishes to the minimum needed at home too.

Random items, like plastic bags and bottles, empty egg cartons, toiletries, buttons and towels, should also be reduced. Before you do, it would be better if you evaluate them and decide whether they should be retained. Ask yourself if they spark joy. If they don't, it would be much better separating ourselves from these things instead of putting them away or hiding them somewhere else "in case" of later.

## 2). Be mindful of what comes into the house or purchases

Reserving your home as a purchase-free household is one of the safest medium for discouraging clutter. How is that possible? You could stop catalogs or advertisements and email notifications on purchases from coming in on your device. Better still, save things you think you really need to get in the Amazon wish list and put it on hold. Wait for some time, then decide later if you still need it.

You will discover that some of those things you thought you urgently needed may turn out to be the last thing on your mind later.

When you go to the store, you must have prepared a list of things you want to buy. With that in mind, you won't be distracted by what you see at the store or during shopping. When you're conscious about what comes into your home, it becomes easier to have your possessions organised. The items in your storage space will be clearly visible to reach, and you can ascertain when something is finished and needs to be refilled. If you are getting good ingredients at the grocery store, it is more stress-free to know what you want to buy, than buying on speculations when you're not even sure if you might be buying extra stuff.

One of the things that you can benefit from thinking carefully about the things you want to buy is that you can plan for your items properly. If you are getting a baby stroller for instance, and you disposed of one during your initial decluttering, you can get a clear picture of what you want this time. But, the only reason you can get that clearer picture is because you were probably aware that the disposed one was a single stroller that wasn't useful. So, going to the store for another one, you can easily decide that you want a double stroller this time around.

What of meals? If your food pantry is well organised, you can tell what items or foodstuff is running low. Then, you can plan how to buy them all at once, instead of purchasing them in bits. You save money, energy and time.

**3). Photo Albums/Digital photos**

Making photo albums for your pictures is a good system of saving memories of your family. The chances of photo albums leading to clutter are low, unlike digital photos. Photo albums are actually easier to access, especially for the kids. Watching them see how much they have grown in those pictures can be very amusing. They will make you appreciate the worth of tying those photos into tangible values.

Digital picture can be hard to take a hold of. They multiply before we even know it, and we tend to get confused or indecisive on how to save them. Instead of staying confused, create a permanent and stable home for them. In this age, a lot of our clutter is mostly digital, but it does not work like that for everyone. You may find digital photos easier to keep than physical photos. If that is your preference, create systems for your digital photos. For instance, there are apps that exist solely for restoring and digitizing old pictures for easy access.

Both physical photo albums and digital photos have their pros and cons, but the point is using them to reduce clutter for your family from the start.

**4). Save those holiday decorations**

There are different means of making your organisation process smooth for holiday decorations:

- Before you pack up the decorations you and your family used for the holiday, examine the ones that were not used, affected by extreme temperatures, pests or broken. If any decoration falls this category, they are better off as 'put-aways'. There is no reason to store them when they are not useful.

- Use plastic bins, customized containers, boxes from your recycle bin, cardboard or empty tins to organise your decorations in those storage spaces properly. Whichever one you use, label them in details. It makes them effortless to figure out which one you kept differently or in the same manner. You could also number the boxes or bins in the order you want to use it next holiday.

- Choose plastic containers and labels to keep the holiday decorations, so it won't take much space in the storage room.

- Do not put too many decorations in a box, so try not to make them too heavy to move around or expose the fragile ones to conditions where they could break.

- Keep the decorations in different locations that suit them. For instance, it would be advisable to place waxy ornaments like candles in humid areas, and store gift wraps in specialty containers, flat under bed storage boxes, or little garbage cans.

- If there is the need to divide the ornaments, do so. You might want to separate the little hooks, wreaths and strings of light from other ornaments, as they could affect the others. The string lights should remain untangled in a different place. The little hooks could be put in zip-lock bags and the wreaths too.

Also, sentimental ornaments in the form of heirlooms could be separately stored. Fragile objects too could be kept with care in thick boxes or special boxes. The Christmas trees can be placed in a different place as well. The trees could be covered with plastic bags, trash bags, or dusted frequently if you can.

- Put the holiday decorations in rooms that are far from the reach of children or pets.

## 5). Decrease the books at home

If your family is into the minimalist style to begin with, it shouldn't come as a surprise if I interject the culture of cutting down on television and leaning towards the value of books instead. Books are good alternatives to television, but they tend to occupy more space in our homes. Instead of waiting for those books to suffocate every part of the house, set up a room for the purpose of a library. There could be boxes placed in the room to give it a library setting. Before arranging the books in that room, dispose any duplicate.

In the same manner, you could give out those books to the nearest library around your house, so you could still go there to read them and read new books of your choice. Either way, your house stays unoccupied with too many books, and you won't lose track of the books in your home.

Similarly, you could make it fun by creating a "Hall of Fame" for the books you love most. If it helps, ask yourself, "Would you buy or search for it again if it got misplaced or burnt in a fire?" If you wouldn't, then you definitely don't need to hold on to it.

## 6). Habitual decluttering

What are the best minimalist strategies that can be used to declutter regularly with your family?

* The first thing to know is to begin and finish with a slow-and-steady approach when organising. Decluttering can be as pressurizing as clutter, if you are in a hurry. It is important that you stay on that middle ground so you don't fall between getting obsessed with decluttering and getting stuck with clutter.

* Use post-it notes for your early stages of organization. It'll help you identify things you labelled quite well.

* Position baskets in your home for returning things you find in the wrong places. That way, it is restrained from becoming clutter. At the end of the day, empty the baskets and return all those things you found.

* Employ eco-friendly multi-taskers. You don't need ten different facilities to clean your bathroom or your kitchen. Two or three all-

purpose cleansers are just fine. For instance, you could use binder clips for tying or holding varying items together. White vinegar and baking soda are multi-purpose cleansers that are applied for tons of things too. These two multi-taskers are both 'green' for the environment, and they simultaneously pare down on the number of bottles and jars as well.

* Make it a habit to give away any of your possessions if you are not using it anymore. Donate them to people who need and value them.

* Tidy up common places and items in the house, e.g., the dishwasher, the kit hen, the floors of your home, the children's toys, the dressers, the bathrooms and so on.

* Shoes are tidier when they are kept at the front door. Rather than kicking them off everywhere, they could be arranged in a designated area or placed in small, snug spaces.

* Stay calm when tidying up. Do not overthink about how to start cleaning. When you are relaxed, the cleaning will be less overwhelming for you.

* When you're done, go through your house with the perspective of a curator or a buyer. Inspect it and work to make it clean. It's so nice like that; why not have it that way for you?

**7). Be flexible about some clutters**

I know this sounds pretty contradicting, because we've been talking about dealing with clutter. I understand that it can be hard overlooking some clutter that you see around the house. But, you need to accept the hard truth, especially when you have kids- they cannot be avoided. Children, if not the rest of the family, are bound to mess up the house while playing. No matter how hard you try, you may not be able to deal with daily clutter that easily. Trying to deal with it might be more or less like dealing with clutter-free; it would be overwhelming.

Instead of getting stuck on decluttering in this circumstance, focus on improvising like cutting down their toys, books and other stuff they play with. You could also discourage the use of junk drawers if you feel the clutter might get extreme. That way, the extent of clutter that messes up the house every day is minimal. Although, you can choose to declutter when they go to sleep or are out of the house completely, if you really can't stand things remaining off balance. Still, it should not get to the point where you get too organised in a way that could affect your relationship with your children. The key is accommodating children, without allowing the clutter to drown your home.

**8). Give each family member a designated space/place/spot to store special keepsakes.**

It could be little spaces on the family's bulletin board for takeout menus, recipe cards, birthday cards, kids' artworks and school paper.

It could even be hooks for each family member to hang his or her coat and bag. And, it could be like a large lidded bin tucked away in an easy-to-access location.

Also, if your family's possessions are scattered around the house, relocate everything to their rooms. You could enjoin everyone to assist in putting the house in order by setting chore charts, time tables or to-do lists for giving out weekly duties. To make it fun and enjoyable, make a playlist to set up the working vibe for the whole family, and other persons there too. Make sure the playlist comprises lively and easy-to-sing-along songs. As everyone sings and dances along, the cleaning gets quicker and fun to do.

# How to get your family on board with a minimalist lifestyle

## Keep a Budget

Maintaining a ritual of having a budget for all money that comes in saves one from clutter. Most clutter that appears is not there by magic. It was all bought and taken into households. So, if there's a lot of clutter in a home, there is a possibility that that family spends a lot. Budgets are not segregated to the financially unstable. It's for everyone. When you plan a budget and work towards it, your chances of becoming more financially secured increases. If your family seems to be having lots of clutter, perhaps you should take a long look at those items. Work on a budget with your family today. Planning a budget pertains to everyone in the family, which is why it is important that everyone participates- including the children. It serves as a check to each other's spending and to deter the desire to get non-essentials.

## Talk to them about the benefits and involve them in decluttering

Interact with them and explain how much minimalism values family, how they can live as a minimalist and how it can be beneficial to them. Do not impose it on them or nag about it; it will only encourage resistance from them. Teach them and let them experience it. When they experience it, they get one step closer to making it their lifestyle.

## Managing holidays and gift-giving when living a minimalist lifestyle

Most families value gifts more than experiences on holidays. Funny enough, most holidays are celebrated doing lots of stressful activities instead of relaxing, reflecting and focusing on sharing love in the family peacefully. Gift-giving is a very nice gesture of portraying love, but it's also the cause of stuff accumulating in many households.

Gift-giving should be limited to material things. They should be redirected to inexpensive activities that give the best experiences. There are so many gift choices to explore as a family. You could give out a museum or membership card to a family for Christmas. Other places to go to include: waterfalls, hiking trails, playgrounds, Disney land, live shows and popular concerts, theatre plays or movies, workshops or classes(martial arts, baking competitions, yoga, swimming, dance classes), spa credits, family games(like scavenger hunts), sporting events, mountaineering or rock climbing, walking tours, fancy restaurants, charities, and the list goes on.

Splurging on activities like this will give you better holidays, because you would be doing things that are less strenuous and clutter-free. However, you need to be specific about the preferred experiences and gifts you want to your family members. Putting them through your preferences will reduce the stress and guilt of discarding thoughtfully-chosen material gifts from the heart. You cannot control the gifts the children receive if you don't carry them along.

Explain your minimalist lifestyle to them and bring up alternative gifts that they could offer, so you do not seem ungrateful. And for every gift received, show your genuine appreciation- even if it does not blend with the lifestyle you are trying to portray for your family. After a while, put away those material gifts. You can donate, exchange or return them later. Furthermore, you could keep the ones that are really loved by your family and you, and then give away the rest. You might want to consider shortening the gift list too.

In the end, the holidays will be enjoyed more when everything is simplified and the focus is only on what is important- what brings joy to the family.

. . . . . . . .

Two renowned minimalist writers: Asha Dornfest and Christine Koh gave an excellent principle of what the words "want", "need" and "love" denote in the world of materialism. When acquiring stuff, we are to ask and answer three honest questions:

Do I want it?

Do I need it?

Do I love it?

    These three questions determine how much value we get from the things we buy. But, the main question that your family should focus on is the third one. Over time, we've talked about minimalism focusing on simplicity, paying full attention to what you love and eliminating what you don't in order to focus on the things you love. As a minimalist family, it should be a custom to prioritize your happiness. How? You concentrate on purchases that would sustain your happiness, not purchases that would only satisfy you for a short period of time, ending up as clutter. That way, your love for stuff and your happiness as a minimalist is equated.

**It's My Favorite Day (2017). Proven Ways to Help Your Family Declutter. Retrieved from**

https://www.itsmyfavoriteday.com/help-family-declutter/

Minimise with me (2018). 10 Tips to Help You Get Your Family On Board With Decluttering. Retrieved from

https://minimisewithme.com/family-and-decluttering/

# CHAPTER EIGHT: DELUTTERING AND RELATIONSHIPS 2: Decluttering As A Minimalist Parent

As a parent, dealing with clutter can be exhausting when handling your children. You have to choose between what they want and what they need. You have to consider and reconsider whether to involve them in decluttering or not. But, what if I told you that you don't have to get confused about any of that anymore?

Organizing the home is something that you, as a parent, can perform with your kids and the rest of the family too. However, everyone should be accountable for their own possessions- including children. The exception is that children need to be supervised, because we all know that, if you ask every child what item they want to let go of while tidying up, they would say none. You can't seriously expect them to toss away any of their toys, unless they are sometimes really unattractive toys (children get easily attracted to colors).

Anyway, children need to be taught the habit of tidying up their rooms and playrooms before anything. Only then can they learn how to dispose of toys they don't need. All the same, you would probably have to do most of the cleaning and monitor the kids while they grow into that culture slowly. I think we need to remind ourselves to not be too organised or obsessed with decluttering in the process. The sole reason for decluttering is to achieve the minimalist lifestyle- which includes keeping only the things they love, not focusing what to discard. The only reason they get discarded in the first place is because we discover they don't love those things anymore. So, forcing your child or any other family member to get rid of their possessions because you feel they are not needed would be wrong. It could even backfire.

How do we get our children interested in decluttering in the minimalist approach then?

**1). Explain your reasons**

We try to share with our kids why we do what we do as much as possible. It's not possible all the time, but we do it whenever we get the chance. If we explain our why, we meet less resistance. Explanations contribute to cajoling them successfully. Explain how minimalism benefits you and the whole family. When we have fewer things in our house, Mommy has more time, is less stressed, and enjoys life more. Point out how much effort cleaning up and organizing so many things takes. Share how clutter makes you feel stressed and unhappy. Your kids may probably not fully appreciate the peace and joy an orderly, clutter-free house can bring, so it's your job to verbalize those feelings and help them understand.

**2). Involve them in the decluttering projects**

Although there are limits to how children can help in decluttering routines, it still pays to get them involved as much as possible. As they grow up, they would get better at it. Teaching them later could be harder, because it can be burdening opening up to things they are not used to. Rather than dealing with that problem in the future, it would be better to build them with that habit from the beginning. Without involving them, our decluttering groove may well go down the drain every time.

Other ways you can involve them in major house duties include:

Make it a family tradition to search for things you don't need and can be donated to charity groups, non-profit organizations and others. When it becomes regular, the kids will get used to it and even want to assist. If they offer to assist by bringing clothes or toys they don't need, accept them.

Create baskets or bins for putting things where they belong. Engage them to work with you in setting those baskets around the house. You could join them in playing sometimes, so you know how they perceive the idea of things getting tidied up. When you play with them on some occasions, gently register it in their minds that their toys and papers should be placed where they belong. Show them how to do it in a fun way. For instance, you could let them make, cut out and paste happy faces on the baskets in the living room or in their playroom for arranging their play things. It would make it easy and fun to tidy things back when they are done playing with them. They basically get first-hand knowledge of how to put things where they belong, when they are involved in placing clutter checkers (baskets, bins).

Ask them questions when you're decluttering. And if you're asking questions, they would be questions that determine whether you should declutter their items or not. I'm taking about questions like: "Do you still love this item?", "Why do you want to keep it?", "What do you love about it?" When you ask those questions consistently with time, they would start learning the whole process and open up to you about things. When they do, congratulate yourself. You invited them to the process and they internalized it successfully!

At other times, it might be best to declutter without them, which leads me to what Marie Kondo said in her recent Netflix show about the possibility of see decluttering with children: "Know when to ignore them." Kids have this funny pattern of turning those neglected toys we decide to put away to their favorite. This was why

I said earlier that children should not be asked about toys they neglected. They would tell you that they love all of them. Instead, put those toys or other play things they have on hold. By putting them on hold, I mean hiding the toys from them, until you are sure that they do not ask for it or miss it in anyway. Then, you can get rid of them.

**3). Respect their sentimental attachment to items**

If your child is sentimental or if he or she is emotionally attached to some items, do not disregard it. You can still declutter with them, but you have to do it slightly different from the usual. Try to understand and create spaces for those sentimental items. Make use of bins that can contain those items with sentimental value. When the bin gets filled, explain to them that they need to let go of some of those things.

Introduce alternatives for your child to express her love for things. For instance, instead of collecting gifts or more objects that could take too much space, you could assist her in planning events and get-togethers or designing cards for people. Even with that, she can still keep her memories and sentiments about things she had or did, but in a different way.

**4). Choosing Toys**

The two major things about choosing toys for your children are: being particular about what kind of toys they should have and how to maintain them. Oftentimes, the first one is not really paid attention to. We are mainly concerned about getting the best toys for our children, as long as they love them. All the same, being specific about the kind of toys your children play with should be important too if you are considering the minimalist lifestyle.

We should be focused on getting few (emphasis on few) quality toys that can serve different purposes for our children. We do not have to give them many toys every time we see one in a birthday party or elsewhere. Kids are not born with the expectations of having excess toys. It's what they are taught while growing up, what they get used to. So, if they start learning how to minimize those toys right from the start, then it would become a habit for them, and you would have less to worry about.

Children can be very loose when it comes to taking care of toys. So, it won't be wrong to say that getting a few durable toys that can last is a better choice compared to having tons of toys that may not survive. The minimalist approach is to buy toys that are high-quality, educational, sustainable and diverse in use (and they have to be obviously pretty too. No child wants to play with unappealing toys). When you set that standard in mind for their toys, they could even last for a long time until the next baby comes or for donations. Not that it's mandatory, but buying toys from resale could be better options for your kids too. Going through resale means those toys are likely strong enough to last for the children.

The second thing is, preserving their toys is a whole different thing entirely. After getting the proper set of toys for your child (ren), there comes the time for them to have them around and the time to purge them. Organizing these toys by rotating what toys should be played with is one of the easiest ways to control possible clutter in your home. Toy rotation minimizes the stress of uncluttering the house after they are done playing.

Toss away toys that are not being used before getting new ones. If your child is simply reluctant, assure him or her that they will be getting better ones if they declutter well. You could even say on their birthdays or Christmas. You'll see how they'll want to organise their toys as quickly as possible.

## 5). Develop a system for organising school papers

School papers are important...no doubt. But, how do we show our children that we value their school memories without them turning to clutter? The fix is to not commit entirely to decluttering; instead, we should focus on minimizing clutter. Celebrate their work on paper, but tame the clutter too.

There are various systems for handling important school papers, but you could create your own or adopt whatever system you prefer. There's the system where you digitalise the papers by taking pictures or scans and attaching them in separate folders, depending on how you classify them or arrange them.

Again, you can save their school papers in a single plastic container or one manila folder for each year. Pretty easy, right? But when it starts overflowing, that's a sign that it needs to be reduced.

Another is to set a clipboard for each child and place all the activities for the day or week-long home assignments, school notes, sport practices, birthday parties, etc. Keep the pressing ones on top and remove the outdated ones for recycling.

These three systems are all effective and check clutter, compared to when we place school papers on the cabinet, table or other surfaces that attract clutter. They undergo frequent purging, which is good too.

Whatever system you develop, it should not be too receptive to space, as it will encourage you to keep filing papers there, until the clutter creeps out and spreads.

## 6). Taking care of the kids' artwork

How do we know what artwork to keep and what to let go of?

Take pictures of the artworks, especially 3D pieces, and create a picture book, portfolio, or folder for them. It's way easier to store them this way than in their actual form.

Recycle or sell them. You could as well remodel and gift them to people as cards or turn them into homemade holiday decorations and book covers.

When it gets too much, go through the artworks with your children, and ask them which ones they love and still want to keep, and which ones they don't like anymore. The whole point is to check what pieces still spark joy. Whichever ones do not spark joy anymore should be disposed.

Place a few of them on the walls of your home. If they start to fade, don't hesitate to take them down. If you're not ready to let them go, because they are such masterpieces, revamp them or furnish them with beautifiers that would complement it.

Store them digitally. Save them in paperless portfolios and folders or organize them with the use of specific apps that are designed for this purpose.

## 7). Give them an incentive to declutter.

When the kids protest items going into the yard sale or donation box, incite them with something to look forwards to. To get them interested in the whole decluttering process, you need to make them see what they will gain from it. For instance, if you tell them that, before they can get to go to the park, a special trip or some other place special (which is a very minimalist thing to do, instead of buying something else that could cause clutter), they would have to tidy up their things for a week. They see the benefit and would want to work towards it. On other hand, it's a win/win- you save space, reduce clutter and get them to participate in decluttering the home. But, using such methods should not be too regular; otherwise, they won't be motivated to tidy up.

. . . . . . . .

As a mom, implementing minimalism with your family can only be successful if you implement it in your life first. You have to lead by example. The first step to doing that is getting honest with yourself. Come clean about every one of your possessions and purge anything that could stop you from living your best life as a minimalist. After tackling your own possessions, then you can focus on your spouse, your children, your grandparents and other members of the family.

If you are quick to be Judge Judy about other people's possessions in the family, you're doing it wrong. You want to grow that minimalist spirit in them? Good. Lead by example. Let them see the benefits and positivity that centers on you as you live the minimalist lifestyle. That does not mean you have to impress them or exaggerate things; just be yourself and allow your life to preach the message to them.

Second, change your mindset. Have you always thought of minimalism as a concept that makes you starve yourself of good clothes, accessories and all? If you still have that mindset or if that thought silently comes up sometimes, kill it. You can't live the minimalist lifestyle if you grow with that thought. Decluttering is not just about getting rid of clothes, dishes and all those random items that clutter your home. It is a means to an end. That end is minimalism. Decluttering is what connects you to minimalism. It is a lifestyle that solely focuses on getting rid of those unnecessary possessions in order to focus on things that make you happy.

Last, start small. Baby steps are very important. I know that starting a new life as a minimalist can be so exciting; I mean there's literally so many things to explore. But, do not be in a hurry. Decluttering as a minimalist is a process, and so is getting your family on board. You can gently nudge them about it, but that's all it should be. Don't be in a hurry to involve them when you're just starting to be a work in progress. Focus on you and your stuff. And if you achieve little successes and goals, reward yourself.

**Francine Jay (2019). Parents. Retrieved from**

**https://www.parents.com/parenting/better-parenting/advice/decluttering-secret-lightly-excerpt-miss-mimimalist/**

**Hollee Actman Baker (n. d.). Organizer Marie Kondo Tackles Children's Artwork Creep. Retrieved from**

**https://www.parents.com/toddlers-preschoolers/everything-kids/organizer-marie-kondo-tackles-childrens-artwork-creep/**

Laura Fenton (n.d.). 12 Real-Mom Ways To Tidy Up Like Marie Kondo. Retrieved from

https://www.parents.com/parenting/home/organisation/real-mom-ways-to-tidy-up-like-marie-kondo/

# CHAPTER NINE: DECLUTTERING AND FINANCES: MINIMALISM AS A FINANCIAL DETOX

It is no doubt that minimalism is basically about living with less. One of its overrated and yet deserving benefits is the financial stability you enjoy from it. Although, the idea of spending less is the most frequent thing that comes to mind, when we talk about its benefits in financial terms. But, that is just one side to it. Minimalism does not just demand that we are intentional about our spending; it solves our financial situations too.

Decluttering and minimalism detox you from unhealthy financial habits and depressing account figures. From eliminating that space taking fax machine that has been used only twice since it was bought, to the lovely second hand car you spend so much money maintaining yet rarely used to living a debt free life after turning down that offer to get that beautiful house situated in the best part of the state yet fantastically far from your place of work on mortgage. Minimalism gives you the financial luxury of having sufficient cash left to register for that new class or invest in a really profitable business opportunity.

Being a minimalist helps you save a lot of money from buying fairly used items, to travelling light, to having a low maintenance home front to the actual decluttering in itself.

**BUYING FAIRLY USED ITEMS**

Buying resale clothing helps to support your minimalist's ultimate goal of a simple, stylish, and minimal wardrobe. Apart from the general and all too popular fears of buying damaged and/or dangerous items, purchasing second-hand items as a minimalist has the following PROS

1. Second-hand items are easy to let go

Cost is usually the primary reason people are hesitant to get rid of things that are no longer of benefit to them. It is like an invisible set of handcuffs that prevents us from getting rid of things.

When you buy something second-hand, you are typically paying 50% (or less) of the actual retail cost, and it is going to be a lot easier to let go of them when they have lived their course.

2. Access to Affordable and Quality Items

Even though investing in a high-quality wardrobe makes sense, especially when you seek to own less, it would be only too normal and expected to struggle with the investment part sometimes. Even when it is within your budget to buy a high ticket item, bringing yourself to spend over $100 dollars for one item of clothing will be hard but you can get this same item for a lesser price with the tag still on it in second-hand shops. Poshmark is a good example of where you can get high-quality fashion items for half the price. You can be confident that you will own these items for years to come (and if you don't, you can most probably part with them guilt-free).

3. Your Guard is up on the Look Out for the Best

Have you ever walked out of a department store with a bag full of items you didn't even mean to buy? The beautiful merchandising and the smell of "brand new" can easily tempt you into buying what you do not need.

When you buy second-hand, you almost have the opposite dynamic. You are looking for reasons NOT to buy so you are on the lookout for evidence of uncleanliness. You read reviews on the seller. You measure your body several times to make sure the item fits. You take extra care in buying because you are buying second-hand, and most times you leave the shop smiling at your purchase. You will have to take care not to buy too much in the heat of the moment. I mean, the goal is minimalism, right? Simplicity and beauty.

4. Wide Range of Style

When you shop at a retail store, you are limited to the items they stock for that season.

When you shop resale, especially online, you can find almost anything you want, stuff much more unique than anything you will be able to find in stores.

By limiting yourself to what stores carry, you might miss out on some really beautiful clothing that is perfect for you.

Talking about buying used items would not be complete without mentioning the financial benefits of used cars. Aside from clothes, there are valid benefits of purchasing a second-hand car, as listed below:

1. Buying a Used Car Saves You Money

On average, used car prices are almost 50% lower than new cars! You will be able to pay off a used car much faster, saving you financing fees. Consumers switch cars at an average of six years after purchase, and if you paid $10,000 for a used vehicle instead of $20,000 for a new one, you could opt into a nicer car for your next vehicle or buy another $10,000 vehicle, creating your very own two for one special!

2. Bulk of Depreciation Has Already Occurred

3. No Exaggerated Fees

A deal on a new car might look great, but many new vehicles have hidden or crazy fees, such as shipping charges, destination fees, and "dealer preparation." Some new car prices include hidden advertising fees that can be as high as $1,000! A used car generally has no hidden fees, but you may still be charged a "doc fee," which can be a few hundred dollars.

4. Lower Customization Costs

You don't have to settle for expensive dealership add-ons when buying a used car. You may install your own at a lower cost than on a new car. What a great way to spend the money you saved when buying a used car.

5. Certified and Thoroughly Inspected

Certified Pre-Owned vehicles assure used car buyers they're getting a quality, thoroughly inspected car that's also a bargain. Certified Pre-Owned vehicles have been inspected, refurbished, and certified by the manufacturer or other certifying authority, assuring the vehicle is high quality. Certified pre-owned vehicles often have an extended warranty, special financing and other benefits. New cars simply hold the assurance that they are new.

6. Warranties

Some used cars still have part of their original warranty. Other used cars may have the option of creating a new warranty. An extended manufacturer warranty on a used car can provide factory trained technicians to repair your car with quality parts and speedy service. Plus, you can utilize a portion of your savings from NOT buying a new car and have a warranty that covers everything until 100,000 miles or more. What new car offers that?

7. Lower Insurance Premiums

If you are in an accident with your new car, the insurance will pay for what the car is worth at that time, leaving a gap between the purchase price and what the vehicle is worth. That's where gap insurance comes in. Gap insurance will cover the difference between what you paid for a new vehicle and what its depreciated value is, but it will raise your insurance premium. Gap insurance isn't necessary with a used car as the depreciation has already occurred.

## 8. Better for the Environment

Almost a quarter of the carbon dioxide a vehicle produces during its life-cycle occurs during manufacturing and initial shipment. Buying a used car reduces the carbon dioxide output into the environment. Used cars also impact the environment less than newer, hybrid vehicles. Hybrid vehicles use lithium-ion, lead-acid, or nickel-metal hydride batteries that have a much larger environmental impact than a used car due to the toxic waste left behind by batteries and acid.

## 9. Lower Annual Registration Fees

In most states, the rate of your annual registration fee is based on your car's value and its model year. Generally, the rate is highest in the first three years, and then levels off after five years. You can save about a thousand dollars by avoiding new and annual registration fees by buying a car that's at least three years old.

**What are the other things you can cut down cost on for the betterment of your financial status?**

## TRAVELING LIGHT

Travelling light, one aspect of the minimalist's life, also goes beyond the bliss of enjoying every bit of your vacation from start to finish because of the lightness of your load and luggage as well as flexibility of changing flights or bus routes. It goes beyond the elimination of stress and time and energy consuming exercises — such as waiting to claim your luggage at the baggage claim, an activity that the JD Powers Study US says each passenger spends an average of 17.3 minutes standing in long lines at airports to get a boarding pass and check luggage. It also affects your financial status and disposition during the journey and experience.

You avoid the cost of your luggage getting damaged, stolen or misplaced by the airline as your luggage will be completely intact with you, overhead your seat in the plane.

You also cut down the cost of replacing property that may go missing if left to be handled by hotel staff. Your kind heart also gets to keep the "change" you would usually give as gratuity.

Travelling light also helps you cut cost on baggage fees. Makes it less likely for you to leave stuff behind and gets you to thinking carefully and smartly before making purchases. And the extra space in your bag makes it easier to carry back some stuff you may find valuable enough to sell back at home for some good money without incurring extra or outrageous extra charges for luggage size.

## LOW MAINTENANCE AND OCCURRENCE OF UNEXPECTED FINANCIAL EXPENSES IN THE HOME FRONT

Minimalism helps discourage excesses, limits the need for things, and makes you likely to need less room, which will make you get a smaller house or living space, leaving you with more money to save on low mortgage or rent.

Having a decluttered home helps prevent common household injury, which though peculiar with the little ones, would do a whole lot of harm to the elderlies living with you, leaving cause for a whole lot of money to be spent in medical care and treatment. And even after this, there is the probability of them being sent to a Home for the Elderly, which may be quite far from home and will incur a lot of cost on taking transport to check up on them regularly.

Having a decluttered home for the Stay at Home Mum with a freelancing job will also promote productivity both at home and in business, as much of her energy won't be spent cleaning up unnecessary and space consuming household appliances regularly. Ignoring clutter is also not a good idea as somehow your mind would be divided between work and your disordered home.

Finding paper work on financial and legal transactions will also prove difficult in a cluttered home and a delay in meeting monthly bill payments, which will in turn incur extra fees for paying past the deadlines, paying extra bucks that would do a lot in other aspects of household maintenance. While you are decluttering this financial mess, take the time to get rid of documents you no longer need and go digital with the rest. This will save you time and make you more efficient in meeting financial obligations.

Clutter also promotes poor air quality and the growth mold that can affect your health. Allergens, germs and vermin can wreak havoc on your body. Poor health affects your work and, in turn, your financial wellbeing.

A general clean-up, reorganization and decluttering can help get you back to your healthy, productive self. Don't let your home kill you or your account balance.

DECLUTTERING IN ITSELF

When decluttering, you will come across heirlooms, gifts and sentimental items you will have a hard time letting go of. It's normal but considering the amount of care and space and time that goes into maintaining that item against its actual benefit to your home it is only inevitable to let go of them. Comically, you really can't wait to let them go as they consume energy and, in some cases, a tax bill.

However, the usual fact that they were left after the death of a loved one can keep one from making this much needed decision. This highly emotional and difficult moment is another reason decluttering is not just an act but a process that requires sufficient mental and emotional preparation.

Before finally giving or selling your Mum's favorite bowl, you are allowed to grieve over them days before they finally go out; this will reduce the feeling of sadness that you expect to creep in after the decluttering. However, a better method would be to sit down and think on these things; are they really worth it?—I mean the emotional attachment and all. With no intention to be hard on you, I am asking once again, "Are they really worth what we usually think they are worth?" Taking your favorite art collection for instance, would you really want your daughter or granddaughter to spend her afternoons cleaning them, believing it is a representation of you? Of course not. Now, how would you feel if she sells it and uses the proceeds to sponsor a new course or her child's camping trip? Sounds fantastic, right? What if she carries them to the local museum for everyone to have and appreciate? Much better, right? Well, the idea is to look for creative ways to give them away that will bring happiness and satisfaction to us and others and do just that.

# WHAT ARE THE BENEFITS OF DECLUTTERING AS A FINANCIAL DETOX

Apart from cutting costs for others who get to have your stuff for free and lowering your tax bills, decluttering in general has the following financial benefits to its credit for you.

## 1. The Organization Is Beneficial – And Contagious

Once you have cleared out unneeded items and get your home organized, you'll find yourself living more efficiently. Things get easier to find, everyday tasks take less time and life just runs more smoothly. That promotes a good attitude that will soon carry over into your work. This positive energy is likely to encourage you to reorganize your finances. This makes you more efficient and productive.

## 2. A More Accurate/Well Detailed Inventory of Properties

While you are deciding what's worth keeping and what's not, it is advisable to take a detailed inventory of what you keep. This not only helps you estimate the value of your belongings, but can be of great value in case of loss, theft, or disaster. Many companies require home inventories in order to cover anything within your home on a claim. An accurate home inventory can make a huge difference when dealing with insurance companies.

## 3. Make Some Extra Money

Many of the items you decide you no longer need may be of value to someone else. When you have decided which things you can live without, have a garage sale and drop the profits into your savings account. There is nothing quite like watching your savings grow into something you can invest with to bring about peace of mind.

## 4. Eliminates Storage Fees

After engaging in the decluttering process once or twice and even more, you may find new storage space in your home. This can translate into less cost for the storage space you need elsewhere.

In fact, decluttering any storage facility you are renting may turn up more items you do not need and need to let go. By the time you are done, you may find you no longer need to pay for storage.

## 5. Eliminate the Risk of Buying Duplicates

A thorough run through of every space in your house will most probably turn up some items you know you had but can no longer find and even those you forgot you had, saving yourself the expense of buying replacements for them or, worse still, more of what you already have. That is more money in the bank.

6. Increase Heating and Cooling Efficiency

Heating and cooling systems depend on air flow to regulate the temperature of your house. Filling the spaces in your house with too much stuff breaks up and restricts air flow. Partially or completely blocking the air ducts makes your heater and air conditioner work harder and increases fuel consumption.

Opening up space will make a noticeable difference in your bills.

7. Downsize

You may be able to downsize. Once you've eliminated the mess, you may find you actually have more living space than you need except you have a large family size. Instead of finding more stuff to fill the empty space, you may have the luxury of considering moving to something more affordable and efficient, an opportunity for a fresh start to go with your new minimalist attitude.

8. Increased Potential Value for your Home

If you're considering selling your home, there's absolutely no better time to get rid of the disorder. Showing an untidy house gives a very bad impression that would leave potential buyers wondering how well the house was cared for if they are walking over your belongings or seeing damaged parts of the house due to excess load pressure. Cleaning up the mess now and even before the need to sell your house will improve your chances of getting the best price.

BONUS TIP: BECOMINGING A MINSUMER.

Advertisers and corporations have defined us as "consumers" encouraging us to buy as much as possible, leaving us working long hours at jobs we used to like to pay for stuff we think we need. Stuff that would be out of style in no time. But, minimalism sets us free from the seemingly endless "work to spend" cycle. We become "minsumers". We minimise our purchases to meet our needs, minimise the impact of our purchases on our personal account and on the people around us. Three words: Reduce, Reuse and Recycle.

**1. Reduce**

"Reducing" is the unsung hero of these three words–I mean, the less we buy in the first place, the less we will need to recycle–"recycle" has become the media darling of campaigns for environmental health and safety as well as financial literacy. We keep forgetting that we would not need to let go of stuff if we had taken proper consideration of their importance and usefulness to us before buying them in the first place.

**2. Reuse**

Reusing is simply using our worn out stuff for purposes other than those they were bought for, which in turn serve such purposes well. This cuts cost. An instance is using a worn out shirt as rag or simply giving away items you're tired of using to others who won't mind using them.

**3. Recycle**

Recycling is usually somewhat like reusing only that, while an item can be reused just as it is, recycling incurs extra expenses for transforming the item into something useable. An instance will be transforming that old Jean trouser into a gown.

· · · · · · · ·

We tend to think we need more belongings to live comfortably than we really do. TV shows, commercials and even our friends – who usually unintentionally determine a subconscious reaction on our part – are constantly showing us new things you shouldn't live without. Taking the time to sort through the items you have accumulated can be a much needed wake up call. Once you start to give up a few unnecessary things, you will realize how little importance they had to begin with.

The change in mindset that comes with this realization can ease the pressure we put on our finances by wanting more. Minimalism helps you find ways to simplify your financial expenses, focus on getting out of debt and staying debt free. You buy less trouble and get more financial security.

**Francine Jay (2010). The Joy of Less, A Minimalist Living Guide: How to Declutter, Organize, and Simplify Your Life.**

**Team RawHide (2015). 9 Advantages of Buying Used Car Instead of a New One. Retrieved from**

https://googleweblight.com/i?u=https://www.rawhide.org/blog/car-tips/9-advantages-of-buying-a-used-car-instead-of-new/&hl=en-NG

Alaya Linton (2019). How Minimalism Can Help or Hurt your Finances. Retrieved from

https://www.thebalance.com/how-minimalism-can-improve-your-finances-4164174

Miriam Caldwell (2019). 8 Ways Minimalism Can Help Your Finances. Retrieved from

https://www.thebalance.com/how-minimalism-can-help-your-finances-4150693

Sheila Beal (2010). Six Savvy Reasons Why You Should Travel Light. Retrieved from

https://googleweblight.com/i?u=https://www.govisithawaii.com/2007/11/26/six-savvy-reasons-why-you-should-travel-light/&hl=en-NG

Cecile (2014). Top 10 Benefits of Traveling Light. Retrieved from http://googleweblight.com/i?u=http://www.thriftyvagabond.com/top-10-benefits-traveling-light/&hl=en-NG

# CHAPTER TEN: After Decluttering, What's next?

With the new trend of decluttering to achieve the minimalist lifestyle, there are so many things to explore and develop. We already know we need to buy less to cut down clutter. We are aware that we need to put away things that do not spark joy in order to live a meaningful life. And we also know that decluttering is not just about getting rid of stuff we don't need, because it carries a lot of weight.

Minimalism and Decluttering are obviously great concepts, but what happens after we take in that knowledge from them and put it to use in our lives? What happens next? When we change our mindset, what phase do we embrace next?

The truth is there is no end. There is no next phase or level that we graduate to after decluttering. We continue to live a life pertaining to minimalism. Decluttering is a process, and Minimalism is a journey. We are to keep living in the process. Stay consistent with the life of simplicity. Keep uncluttering and focusing on things we value. There is no such thing as perfection after we achieve that dreamy, uncluttered space. The key to these two concepts is patiently maintaining that sense of organization. We are to stick to the decision of owning less every day of our lives. In short, establish a long-term routine for yourself.

# CONCLUSION

Now, you have come to appreciate minimalism for what it is through decluttering, you may still be wondering "What exactly is the difference between both terms?" In simple terms, minimalism is not decluttering, but it starts with decluttering sustained by determination, reason, understanding, passion, consistency and creativity combined with basic financial intelligence and subjective taste. That is the difference. One is a method, the other, a lifestyle.

Minimalism centers on downsizing the number of your material possessions to only the basic essentials of life. Decluttering, on the other hand, is regarded as a principle applied to keeping the home clean and maintaining that cleanliness by uncluttering unnecessary items continuously. They both reward you with abundance of time to pursue anything- your goals, new experiences, happiness, contentment, family, and so much more.

Decluttering and Minimalism go hand in hand, but they should not be taken as the same thing. You can declutter and not be a minimalist. For instance, I could reduce the clutter in my room because I want my room to look more organised. I may also remove all the clutter in my room till it transits to simplicity. The former is a lifestyle, while the latter is an act. Decluttering can be carried out without minimalism. But most of the time, they go together because carrying out decluttering in your home is the journey to minimalism. It is an action that leads to living the best minimalist lifestyle.

Decluttering differs from Minimalism, but the only exception is where these two concepts meet as a means to an end. The desire for people to declutter is what leads to minimalism most of the time. Enough said.

Printed in the USA
CPSIA information can be obtained
at www.ICGtesting.com
LVHW010913100324
774064LV00007B/640